Maths Action Plans

Solving Problems and Handling Data

Y6/P7

David Clemson and Wendy Clemson

Contents

Introduction and planning	v
Curriculum planner, differentiation and assessment	vi
The MAPs lesson	vii
Scottish correlations	viii

Autumn term

Unit 1   Money problems — 1

- Lesson 1   Use multiplication and division to solve money problems (single-step). Explain working — 2
- Lesson 2   Use division to solve money problems (single-step). Explain working. Check by estimating — 3
- Lesson 3   Use all four operations to solve money problems (single-step and multi-step). Choose appropriate operation and calculation methods. Explain working. Check by estimating — 5
- Supplementary activities — 6

Unit 2   Handling data — 7

- Lesson 1   Use language of probability, including events with two or more equally likely outcomes — 8
- Lesson 2   Use language of probability, including events with two or more equally likely outcomes — 10
- Lesson 3   To extract, present and interpret discrete grouped data on a bar chart — 11
- Lesson 4   To extract, present and interpret discrete grouped data on a bar chart — 13
- Lesson 5   Use prepared computer database to compare presentations of data — 14
- Lesson 6   Use prepared computer database to compare presentations of data — 15
- Lesson 7   Find the mode and range of a set of data. Begin to find median — 16
- Lesson 8   Find the mode and range of a set of data. Begin to find median and mean — 17
- Supplementary activities — 18

Unit 3   Measures problems, including time — 20

- Lesson 1   Use all four operations to solve measurement problems involving length. Choose appropriate operations and calculation methods. Explain working — 21
- Lesson 2   Use all four operations to solve measurement problems involving length. Choose appropriate operations and calculation methods. Explain working — 22
- Lesson 3   Use all four operations to solve time problems. Choose appropriate operations and calculation methods. Explain working — 23
- Lesson 4   Use all four operations to solve time problems. Choose appropriate operations and calculation methods. Explain working — 24
- Supplementary activities — 25

Unit 4   "Real-life" problems — 26

- Lesson 1   Use all four operations to solve "real-life" problems. Choose appropriate operations and calculation methods. Explain working — 27
- Lesson 2   Use all four operations to solve "real-life" problems. Choose appropriate operations and calculation methods. Explain working — 28
- Supplementary activities — 29

Spring term

Unit 5   Money problems   30
- Lesson 1   Use all four operations to solve money problems. Choose appropriate operations and calculation methods. Explain working   31
- Lesson 2   Use all four operations to solve money problems. Choose appropriate operations and calculation methods. Check by using inverse operation including with calculator   32
- Lesson 3   Use all four operations to solve money problems. Choose appropriate operations and calculation methods. Check by using inverse operation including with calculator   33
- Supplementary activities   34

Unit 6   Measures problems   35
- Lesson 1   Use all four operations to solve measurement problems involving grams and kilograms. Choose appropriate operations and calculation methods. Explain working   36
- Lesson 2   Use all four operations to solve measurement problems involving grams and kilograms. Choose appropriate operations and calculation methods. Explain working   37
- Supplementary activities   39

Unit 7   Handling data   40
- Lesson 1   Represent, extract and interpret data in a line graph. Recognise that intermediate points have meaning   41
- Lesson 2   Represent, extract and interpret data in a line graph (involving conversion, e.g. miles to kilometres). Recognise that intermediate points have meaning   42
- Lesson 3   Represent, extract and interpret data in a line graph. Recognise that intermediate points have meaning   43
- Supplementary activities   45

Unit 8   "Real-life" problems   46
- Lesson 1   Use all four operations to solve word problems involving "real life". Choose appropriate operations   47
- Lesson 2   Use all four operations to solve word problems involving "real-life" measurement. Choose appropriate operations and calculations   48
- Lesson 3   Collect data to use in solving "real-life" problems   49
- Lesson 4   Use all four operations to solve word problems involving "real-life" measurement. Choose appropriate operations and calculations. Check by adding in reverse order, including with a calculator   50
- Supplementary activities   51

Summer term

Unit 9   Money problems   52
- Lesson 1   Use all four number operations to solve word problems involving money including finding percentages   53
- Lesson 2   Use all four number operations to solve word problems involving money. Use a calculator or written method to convert foreign currency   54
- Lesson 3   Use all four number operations to solve word problems involving money. Calculate simple percentages, such as VAT, using a calculator   55
- Supplementary activities   57

Unit 10   Handling data   58

Lesson 1	Extract information from a simple frequency table.	59
Lesson 2	Extract information from a simple frequency table and convert data to percentages, using a calculator	60
Lesson 3	Solve a problem by representing, extracting and interpreting data in a bar line graph	61
Lesson 4	Recognise a simple pie chart. Interpret sections on a simple pie chart. Calculate totals represented on a pie chart. Draw a simple pie chart	62
Lesson 5	Recognise a simple pie chart. Interpret sections on a simple pie chart. Calculate totals represented on a pie chart. Calculate values on a pie chart as a percentage	63
Lesson 6	Recognise a simple pie chart. Interpret sections on a simple pie chart. Calculate totals represented on a pie chart. Calculate values on a pie chart as a percentage	64
Lesson 7	Solve a problem by representing, extracting and interpreting data on a pie chart	65
Lesson 8	Consolidate previous work on frequency tables and pie charts	66
Supplementary activities		68

Unit 11   Measures problems   69

Lesson 1	Use all four operations to solve measurement problems. Choose appropriate operations and calculations. Explain working	70
Lesson 2	Use all four operations to solve measurement problems. Choose appropriate operations and calculations. Explain working	71
Lesson 3	Understand there are different time zones around the world. Use all four operations to solve time problems. Choose appropriate operations and calculations. Explain working	72
Lesson 4	Understand there are different time zones around the world. Use all four operations to solve time problems. Choose appropriate operations and calculations. Explain working	73
Supplementary activities		74

Unit 12   "Real-life" problems   75

Lesson 1	Use all four operations to solve "real-life" word problems. Calculate percentages of amounts. Explain working	76
Lesson 2	Use all four operations to solve "real-life" word problems. Calculate percentages of amounts. Choose appropriate operations. Explain working	77
Lesson 3	Use all four operations to solve "real-life" word problems. Choose appropriate methods and calculations. Explain working	78
Supplementary activities		79

Resources sheets 1–66   80–145

General resource sheets A–G   146–152

Introduction

Maths Action Plans (MAPs) is a series of practical teacher's resource books, four for each year of the primary school from Year 3/P4 to Year 6/P7. Each book contains lesson plans designed to help you to plan and deliver well-structured lessons in line with the National Numeracy Strategy *Framework for Teaching Mathematics* (1999).

MAPs is different from other lesson-plan based resource books because each title in the series focuses upon a different strand of mathematics at a particular year, thereby offering you a more coherent, "joined-up" approach to the teaching of key mathematical concepts. The activities in this book cover the following mathematical topics within the "Solving problems" and "Handling data" strands:

- problems involving "real life", money and measures (including time)
- organising and interpreting data.

While the lessons are designed to offer support across a strand, links to other strands are made clear throughout. For example, "Using and applying mathematics" underpins all three National Curriculum attainment targets. There are three aspects of "using and applying" covered by the contents of this book:

- problem solving
- communicating
- reasoning.

Within each aspect, children have to:

- organise
- select/decide
- explain/justify
- make connections
- try different approaches.

The MAPs lessons will encourage the children to organise their thinking about problems, select appropriate operations, explain their reasoning and suggest alternative methods. Lessons addressing other strands in the mathematics curriculum, that is "Measures, Shape and Space"; "Number" and "Calculations", can be found in companion titles in this series.

Planning – adopting or adapting

Although these books focus on specific mathematics topics, they also offer a bank of lessons that give complete coverage in line with the *Framework for Teaching Mathematics Sample Medium Term Planner* (2000). Every objective is tackled and the number of lessons matches the number of lessons in the planner exactly. This means that MAPs can be used as a complete core mathematics programme. Alternatively, the lessons can be used as additional plans for an existing scheme of work. Where fresh ideas or alternative approaches are desired then the lessons in MAPs can fit the bill.

To adapt or personalise the MAPs lessons to meet your needs, you might consider the following actions:

- select and copy individual MAPs lessons or units to supplement lessons/units that you have already
- add your own prepared resources to those recommended in the plans
- check that the lessons match the needs of children in your class and if necessary substitute lessons for MAPs lessons from other years for more or less confident children
- work on the first lessons of a unit, then plan the use of supplementary activities as a stimulus for extension work or as the starting points for subsequent whole-class lessons.

The intention throughout is to provide fresh ideas for planning the content, pace and pitch of your lessons within a framework that can be adopted or adapted to meet your needs and the needs of your class.

Curriculum planner

The lessons in this book have been written in line with the *Framework for Teaching Mathematics Sample Medium Term Planner* (2000).

The opening page of each unit includes the following information, which can be used in your medium term plans:

Framework links
This chart highlights the coverage of the NNS objectives and establishes the expectations of the unit.

Setting the scene
This section highlights the ideas underpinning the unit and any key mathematical concepts that are emphasised in the unit.

Starting points
This section identifies the knowledge and mathematical skills that children should have attained before tackling the lessons of this unit.

Checking progress
This section includes broad descriptions of expected outcomes by the end of the unit. It also offers insight into what children might know and be capable of doing if they have gone above or below these expected outcomes.

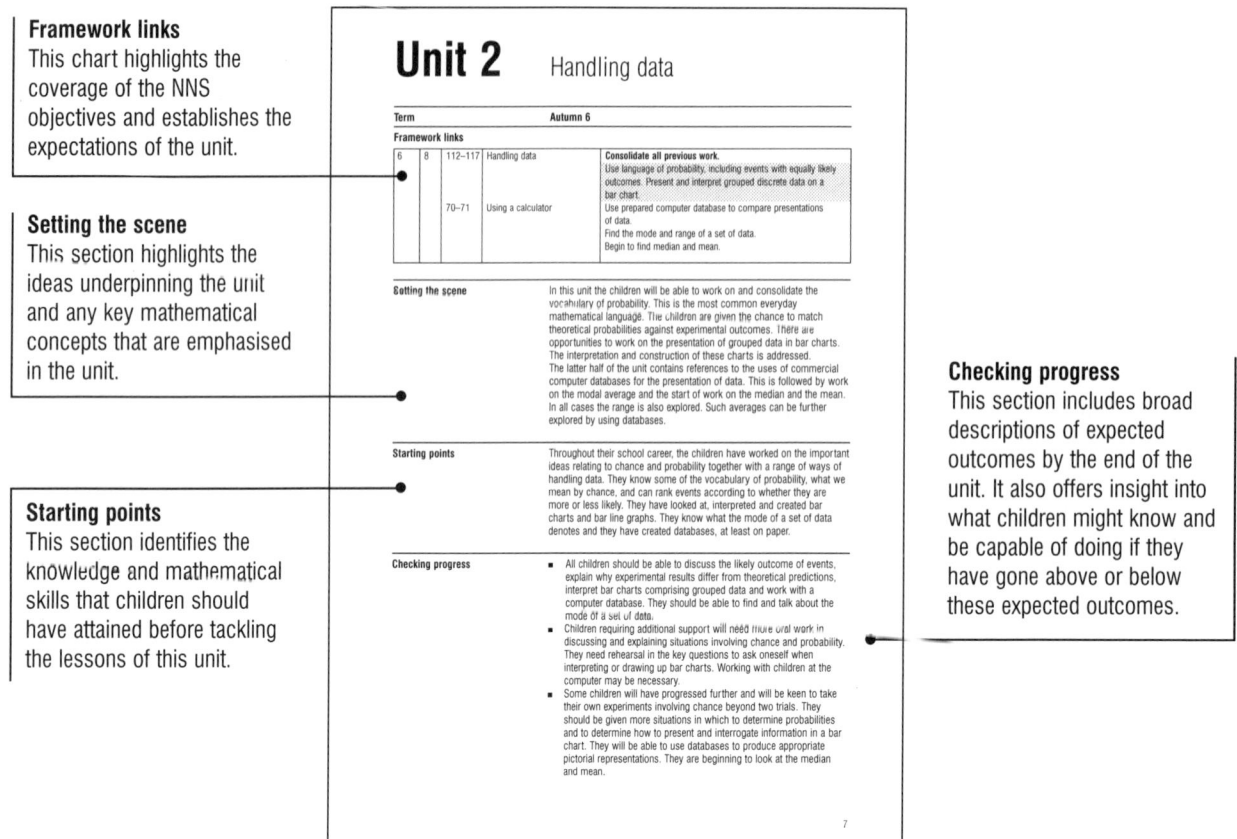

For each topic area, the MAPs have been carefully planned to ensure that lessons meet the requirements of teachers in Scotland and Wales given in the attainment targets both for *National Guidelines 5–14* in Scotland and in *Mathematics in the National Curriculum in Wales*. A correlation chart for *National Guidelines 5–14* in Scotland is presented on page viii. A correlation chart for *Mathematics in the National Curriculum in Wales* can be accessed on the following website: www.nelsonthornes.com/primary

Differentiation

MAPs offers a controlled level of differentiation, as the National Numeracy Strategy recommends. This can be by task, through assessed outcomes and/or suggestions for planning on the basis of prior knowledge or experience. In some cases whole-class lessons are offered with "escape points"; in other cases there are lessons with differentiated resource sheets or lessons where "support" or "challenge" ideas offer an alternative route for individuals, pairs or groups.

Assessment

The learning objectives for each lesson are clearly stated and assessment opportunities are offered throughout in many of the pupil activities and resource sheets. Make time to observe the children as they work at these tasks during the main part of the lesson. Identify whether children have understood the concept or whether they have any misconceptions that need to be addressed. You might, at this stage, plan the use of additional support or challenge materials identified in each plan.

During the plenary, key questions are offered to provide important assessment information to guide teaching and planning. These should be supplemented by the use of open questions such as *How did you work that out?*, *What if … ?* and *Are there other ways of working this out?*

Finally, for medium term assessment, additional tasks can be planned for individual pupils or small groups during the half-termly "assess and review" lessons by using pupil activities or the supplementary activities at the end of each unit.

The MAPs lesson

The plans are intended as a support for the daily mathematics lesson for the school mathematics co-ordinator, teacher and classroom assistant working within a particular group. Each lesson includes the following sections:

Learning objectives
This section gives the explicit targets for each lesson including oral and mental starters.

Mental/oral starter
This shows the balance of oral and mental objectives across each title. Some are free-standing, others link to the main activity.

Main activity
Detailed guidance is given here which covers the main part of each lesson, including a description and organisation of the activity and a range of ideas for differentiating each lesson. Key questions are highlighted in italics.

Unit 3 Lesson 4

Lesson 4

Learning objectives
Mental/oral starter:
- Convert between km, m, cm, and mm and vice versa

Main teaching activities:
- Use addition, subtraction, multiplication and division to solve time problems
- Choose appropriate operations
- Explain how they worked them out

Resources
Photocopy Resource Sheet 22 onto thin card (It would be useful to double the size of the cards. Cut out the individual cards ready for the mental/oral starter.), a "washing line" and pegs (The washing line should stretch across the classroom in front of the children. Clip the pegs along its length.), an OHT of Resource Sheet 23, photocopies of Resource Sheet 23, pocket train timetables (These should be collected beforehand from the local station.)

Vocabulary
km, m, cm, mm, time, minute, hour, method, calculation, operation, addition, subtraction, multiplication, division

MENTAL/ORAL STARTER 10

Erect a "washing line" with pegs on it across the classroom. Place all the measure cards on the table. Hold up one or two to show the children that each has a measurement on it in kilometres, metres, centimetres or millimetres. Invite individual children to peg the cards in size order along the line. Discuss what is happening and ask other children to offer the necessary conversions so that comparisons of the measurements can be made.

MAIN ACTIVITY 40

Whole class, pairs

Discuss why it is that we need timetables and ask the children key questions to test their understanding.

What does a timetable tell us?

What are the two sets of information presented on a timetable?

Why is it called a timetable?

Display the OHT of Resource Sheet 23 so that all the children can see it clearly. Talk through what it presents. Show the inward and outward journey, the departure times and indicate where the arrival and departure times differ. Answer any questions that the children may have about the interpretation of the timetable.

Give each pair of children a copy of Resource Sheet 23. They should work on the challenges together and then each make a record of the work they have done in their workbooks.

Support
Help the children who find the timetable too complex to look at it a section at a time. They can work out the time taken from each station to the next. If these are written on a group chart of the journey, they will then find it easier to solve the problems.

Challenge
Allow the children to look together at a real pocket timetable and see if they can interpret it.

PLENARY 10

Show again the OHT of Resource Sheet 23. Take each challenge in turn and ask the children how they worked it out. Compare the methods the children have used.

Key fact or strategy
To read a timetable we need to look at the information that is set across and down the table.

24

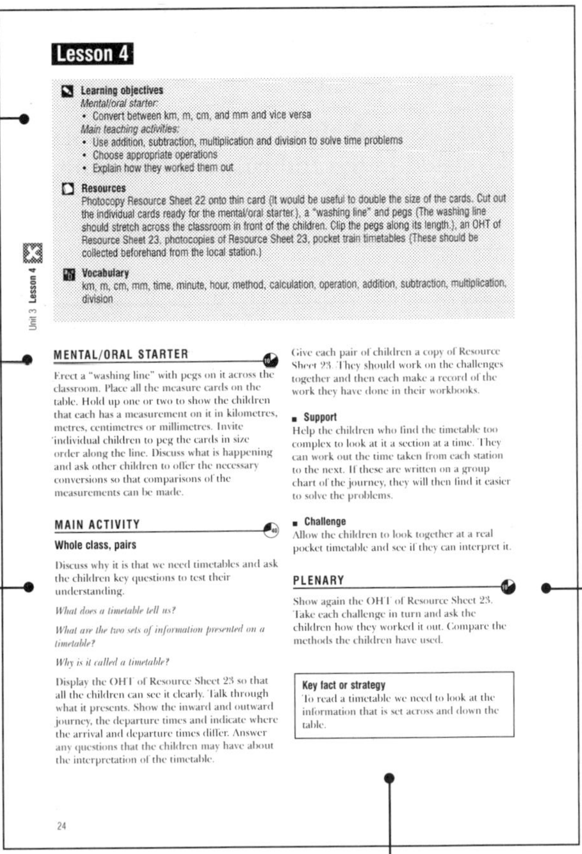

Plenary
Key questions are highlighted here in italics to guide the structure of each plenary session. Opportunities are provided to assess pupils' progress and compare strategies used. Each plenary will help you to guide outcomes referenced to the learning objectives of the lesson.

Key fact or strategy
This section provides a summary of key facts learned or strategies that the children might have used. It also includes links to other areas of mathematics or to applications in other subjects including practical, everyday applications.

Supplementary activities

Fresh ideas are provided here, with further exemplification, different approaches, homework opportunities ...

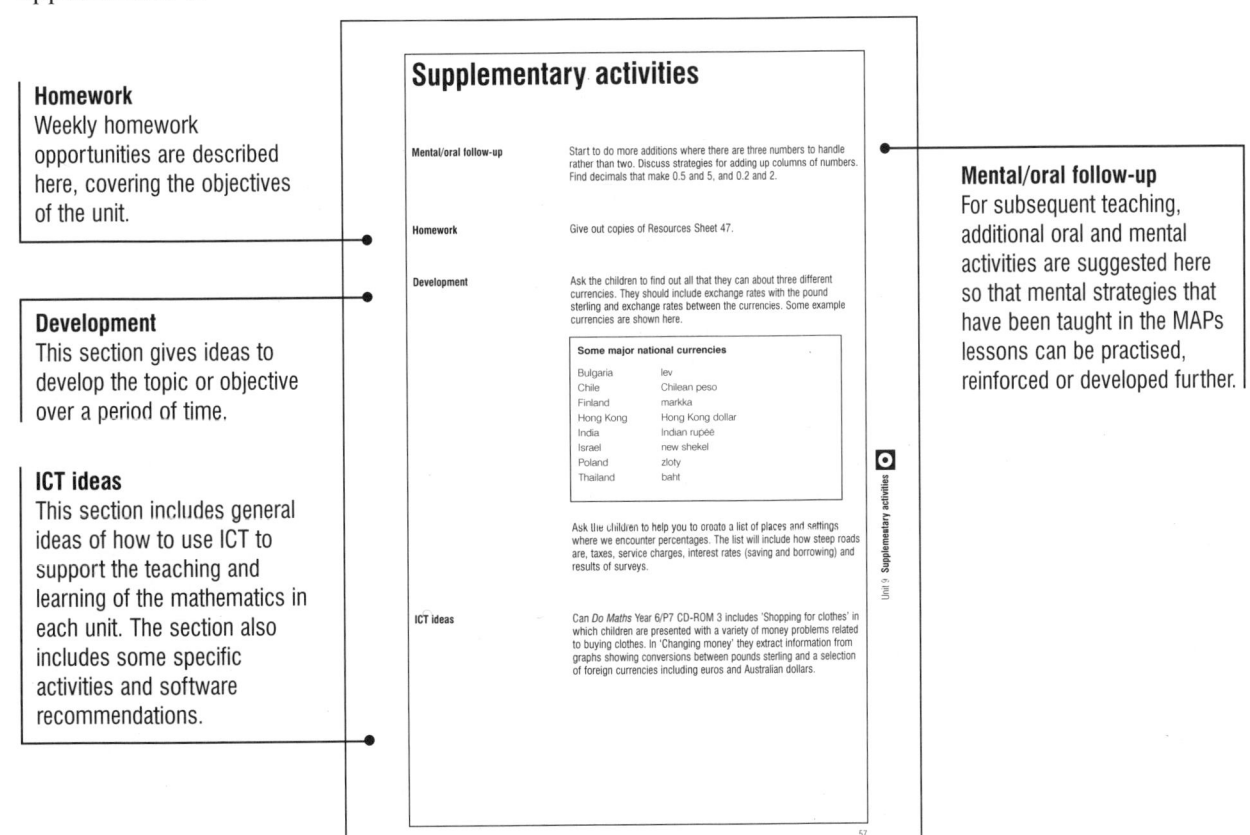

Homework
Weekly homework opportunities are described here, covering the objectives of the unit.

Development
This section gives ideas to develop the topic or objective over a period of time.

ICT ideas
This section includes general ideas of how to use ICT to support the teaching and learning of the mathematics in each unit. The section also includes some specific activities and software recommendations.

Supplementary activities

Mental/oral follow-up Start to do more additions where there are three numbers to handle rather than two. Discuss strategies for adding up columns of numbers. Find decimals that make 0.5 and 5, and 0.2 and 2.

Homework Give out copies of Resources Sheet 47.

Development Ask the children to find out all that they can about three different currencies. They should include exchange rates with the pound sterling and exchange rates between the currencies. Some example currencies are shown here.

Some major national currencies

Bulgaria	lev
Chile	Chilean peso
Finland	markka
Hong Kong	Hong Kong dollar
India	Indian rupee
Israel	new shekel
Poland	zloty
Thailand	baht

Ask the children to help you to create a list of places and settings where we encounter percentages. The list will include how steep roads are, taxes, service charges, interest rates (saving and borrowing) and results of surveys.

ICT ideas Can *Do Maths* Year 6/P7 CD-ROM 3 includes 'Shopping for clothes' in which children are presented with a variety of money problems related to buying clothes. In 'Changing money' they extract information from graphs showing conversions between pounds sterling and a selection of foreign currencies including euros and Australian dollars.

Unit 9 Supplementary activities

57

Mental/oral follow-up
For subsequent teaching, additional oral and mental activities are suggested here so that mental strategies that have been taught in the MAPs lessons can be practised, reinforced or developed further.

Scottish correlations

In this curriculum planner chart, no reference has been made to the activity at the beginning of each lesson in this book, namely the mental/oral starter. These are designed to augment the numeracy and mathematical understanding of the children. They are wide-ranging and often address different objectives from those set down for the main activities of each lesson. It is possible for teachers in Scottish schools to select from the mental/oral starters those which match their pupils' learning and teaching needs.

Additionally, at the end of each unit of this book there are supplementary activities, and suggestions for using ICT. These will support work related to the Information Handling Target and the Number, Money and Measurement Attainment Target.

Scottish guidelines planner

Information handling attainment target

Strands	Level C	Level D	Level E
Collect		Select information sources *Unit 8*	Select sources for practical experiments *Unit 8*
Organise	Enter data in a table *Unit 2*	Use a database or spreadsheet table *Unit 2*	Design and use diagrams and tables *Unit 2* Design and use a database/spreadsheet *Unit 2*
Display		Construct graphs *Units 2, 10*	Construct straight line/curved graphs for continuous data *Unit 7* Construct pie charts for percentages *Unit 10*
Interpret		From a range of displays and databases – retrieve subject to one condition *Unit 2*	From a range of displays and databases – retrieve subject to one condition *Unit 2* Describe main features of a graph *Unit 7* Calculate mean *Unit 2*

Number, money and measurement attainment target

Strands	Level C	Level D	Level E
Money		UK coins/notes to £20 plus, exchange *Unit 9*	Relationships between currencies *Unit 9*
Add and subtract		Applications in number, measurement, money *Units 1, 3, 4, 5, 6, 8, 9, 11, 12*	Applications in number, measurement, money *Units 1, 3, 4, 5, 6, 8, 9, 11, 12*
Multiply and divide	Applications in number, measurement, money to £20 *Units 1, 3, 4, 5, 6, 8, 9, 11, 12*	Applications in number, measurement, money *Units 1, 3, 4, 5, 6, 8, 9, 11, 12*	Applications in number, measurement, money *Units 1, 3, 4, 5, 6, 8, 9, 11, 12*
Round numbers			Round any number to one decimal place *Unit 1*
Fractions, percentages and ratio			With calculator find fraction/percentage of a quantity *Unit 9*
Time		24-hour timetable *Unit 11*	

Unit 1 Money problems

Term				Autumn 2–3	
Framework links					
2–3	10	52–57	Understanding × and ÷	Consolidate all previous work. Understand and use relationships between the 4 operations, and the principles of the arithmetic laws.
		60–65	Mental calculation strategies (× and ÷)	Use related facts and doubling or halving, for example, halve an even number, double the other; multiply by 25, by × 100, then ÷ by 4. Approximate first.
		66–69	Pencil and paper procedures (× and ÷)	Use informal pencil and paper methods to support, record or explain × and ÷. Extend written methods to ThHTU × U and short multiplication involving decimals.
		82–85	Money and "real-life" problems	Use all four operations to solve money or "real-life" word problems.
		70–75	Making decisions and checking results including using a calculator	Choose appropriate operations/calculation methods. Explain working. Check by estimating. Use inverse operation, including with a calculator.

Setting the scene

This unit provides the opportunity for the children to continue to practise working with problems involving money. Most children will be applying the mathematical principles that they know in "real-life" situations, so practice with realistic problems is invaluable. While the mathematical ideas in this unit should be familiar to the children, there is an attempt to present them in a variety of settings.

Starting points

In Year 5/P6 the children will have continued to hone their skills in working with money and "real-life" problems. They will have worked on the idea that there are often a number of ways to solve a problem and they will be able to explain their own ways of working things out. They will be familiar with estimation and why it can be useful.

Checking progress

- All children should be able to use addition, subtraction, multiplication and division when working on problems involving money.
- Children requiring additional support will need resources and supervision when coping with the interpretation of problems (What do I need to do? What operations will I be using here?). They will benefit from extra practice in solving the kinds of problem that they, as individuals, find difficult.
- Some children will have progressed further and will be able to devise other problems that require similar operations in their solution.

Lesson 1

Learning objectives

Mental/oral starter:
- Add pairs of two-digit numbers including crossing 100

Main teaching activities:
- Use multiplication and division in solving single-step money problems
- Explain how they did the working out
- Record the problem and its solution using numbers, signs and symbols

Resources
An OHT of Resource Sheet 1 (Photocopies of Resource Sheet 1 may be required for some children as a Challenge activity.), photocopies of Resource Sheet 2, a box of facsimile sterling coins and notes (for Support)

(Note: As an additional resource for children who require extra support, the images on Resource Sheet 1 can be enlarged and photocopied separately for mounting on card. The children can then lay in front of them the items that they need.)

Vocabulary
Two-digit, addition, calculation, total cost, multiplication, division

MENTAL/ORAL STARTER

Ask a child to give you their date of birth and write this up on the board, for example, 27 October 1991. Use the numbers generated to create some two-digit additions. By using the date in this example, they would include: 27 + 19, 27 + 99 and 19 + 91.

Write the number sentences on the board and ask individual children for the answers. Discuss the possible ways of working them out. Invite another child to give you their birth date, and use the numbers in that to create more two-digit additions. Repeat this exercise several times.

MAIN ACTIVITY

Whole class, individuals, pairs

Place the OHT of Resource Sheet 1 on the projector. Point to one of the items and match it with one of the prices. Any of the prices shown can be indicated. If, for example, the spoon and £1.50 are chosen, these can be ringed with a washable OHT pen. Then say:

One spoon costs one pound fifty. How much do 2 spoons cost?

How much do 4 spoons cost? ... 10 spoons?

In each case work the calculation through. Ask the children for suggestions about how the calculations should be written up on the board. Incorporate their ideas into the written examples.

Choose other items and prices and help the children to work out the cost of multiples of the items.

Use the same OHT but now find the costs of single items.

Ten clothes pegs cost 90p. How much does each cost?

Two tea towels cost £5.60. How much does each one cost?

Again work through the kind of calculation necessary and write it up on the board.

Give a copy of Resource Sheet 2 to each child and allow them time to work through the calculations. When they have completed the work they can check through their answers with a partner.

■ Support
The children may benefit from setting out the costs of the items by using notes and coins. Use appropriate questioning to help them to decide on a strategy for solving the problems.

What kind of calculation do you need to do?

What happens when we multiply?

What happens when we multiply, say, nine pounds fifty, by ten?

How do we write out this multiplication?

■ **Challenge**
Give the pairs of children a copy of Resource Sheet 1 and invite them to use the items and prices to create some multiplication and division problems.

> **Key fact or strategy**
> Determine the operation to be used when tackling a single-step problem.

PLENARY

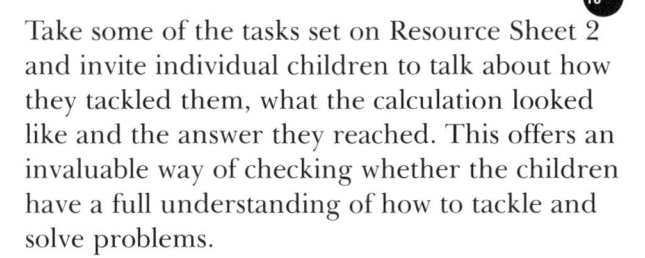

Take some of the tasks set on Resource Sheet 2 and invite individual children to talk about how they tackled them, what the calculation looked like and the answer they reached. This offers an invaluable way of checking whether the children have a full understanding of how to tackle and solve problems.

Lesson 2

Learning objectives
Mental/oral starter:
- Find pairs of numbers that sum to 100
- Find pairs of decimals that sum to 10
- Find pairs of decimals that sum to 1

Main teaching activities:
- Use division in solving single-step money problems
- Solve multi-step money problems
- Explain how they did the working out
- Check by making estimates

Resources
Three lists of numbers, as shown below (The lists of numbers can be written on sheets of paper and kept covered until needed for the mental/oral starter.), brochures or junk mail showing special offers at a local grocery store, a box of facsimile sterling coins and notes (for Support), photocopies of Resource Sheet 3

Vocabulary
Sum, pair, decimal place, fraction, calculate, price, half, third, division, quarter

MENTAL/ORAL STARTER

Write on the board a list of numbers between 0 and 100 (see sample List 1). Ask individual children in turn, and in quick-fire succession, to say what the pair number is that should be added to each of the numbers to make 100.

Write a second list of numbers between 0 and 10, with one or two decimal places (see sample List 2). See if the children can call out the numbers that need to be added to each of these to make 10.

Next ask all the children to think of a decimal number between 0 and 1. As each child says their number in turn, help the children to work out what needs to be added to this number to make 1. Write List 3, as shown below, on the board and, with the children's help, link up the pairs of numbers.

95	7.5	0.25
78	2.3	0.5
62	5.4	0.75
36	7.25	0.90
84	2.1	0.82
51	9.35	0.7
19	4.02	0.01
23	1.25	0.10
List 1	**List 2**	**List 3**

MAIN ACTIVITY

Whole class, individuals, small groups

Show the children the special offer brochures. Discuss the idea of special offers: three for two, buy one get one free, and so on. Inspect these to determine what fraction of the price paid can be calculated as the price of one item.

Write £26.60 on the board and ask the children what half of this would be. Write £12.82 and ask for half of that. Ask the children how they worked out the answers.

Write £24.36 on the board and ask what a third of it is. Finish by writing £12.48 and ask for a third of this amount. Tell the children that their work today will focus on special offers and fractions of sums of money (that is, mostly division problems).

Give each child a copy of Resource Sheet 3. Allow the children time to do the first two sets of problems. They should then share their methods of working with a classmate.

■ **Support**

Allow the children to work in pairs on the whole task. Re-visit them frequently to check that they fully understand the methods they are using and can talk about their working out.

■ **Challenge**

Ask the children, in pairs, to explore how to find the original price if one quarter has been taken off. Here are some suggested prices and a note about some of the thinking worked through.

£9.72   £4.80   £2.67   £171.06

(Note: To work out the original price when a quarter has been taken off, the children will have to appreciate that we need to share the reduced price into three equal parts, for example, £9.72 is £3.24 + £3.24 + £3.24 when split in this way. This represents ¾ of the original price so we need to add another ¼ that is £3.24 to £9.72 to get the original price of £12.96.)

PLENARY

Go through the two Resource Sheet 3 challenges that have been completed. Ask the children to offer estimates of the likely answers to serve as checks for work done. Here is an example.

Shower gel costs £1.38. If Mick buys one and gets one free we can estimate the cost for each by saying, £1.38 is approximately £1.40. Half of £1.40 is 70p (and this is easier to determine in our heads than half of £1.38). Our answer should be almost 70p.

Work through the final set of challenges on Resource Sheet 3 with the children. Talk about the methods of working out that may be used.

> **Key fact or strategy**
> Halving and finding thirds and quarters is a skill that is useful when working out the prices of special offers in everyday life.

Unit 1 Lesson 2

Lesson 3

Learning objectives
Mental/oral starter:
- Give pairs of factors for numbers up to 100

Main teaching activities:
- Use addition, subtraction, multiplication and division to solve single-step and multi-step money problems
- Explain how they worked them out
- Check by making estimates

Resources
A bank of numbers for the mental/oral starter (There are some examples on Resource Sheet 4 and this can be made into an OHT for whole-class use or photocopied with ×4 magnification to yield a number chart for the class.), photocopies of Resource Sheet 5, slips of paper (for Challenge)

Vocabulary
Factor, pair, cost, add, subtract, multiply, divide, calculate, estimate

MENTAL/ORAL STARTER

Show the children the bank of numbers either as an OHT or on a display sheet. Invite individuals to name two factors for each of the numbers, other than 1 and the number itself. Ask which numbers have more than two pairs of factors, for example, the number 48 has the following factor pairs: 24 and 2, 12 and 4, 6 and 8, 3 and 16.

MAIN ACTIVITY

Whole class, individuals

Use a couple of items from Resource Sheet 5 to set the scene for the lesson, for example, posters and cassette tapes. Draw the items on the board and give them prices. Tell the children:

The music store has posters at £3.45 and cassette tapes at £2.60.

Ask the children questions that they can try orally, before working through the answers on the board.

What is the cost of 2 posters?

What is the cost of 4 cassette tapes?

What is the cost of a poster and a cassette tape?

What is the change from £15 if I buy 2 of each?

Give out copies of Resource Sheet 5 and ask the children to complete it individually.

Support
The children would benefit from more practice at one-step problems based on the prices of the items in the music store list.

Challenge
The children can be given two strips of paper on which they should write out two more challenges like the ones that they have just done. The slips of paper can then be exchanged with classmates so that they solve each other's challenges.

PLENARY

Take each challenge from Resource Sheet 5 in turn and work it out on the board. Discuss with the children how they have tackled the problem. In each case, look at the value of estimating the answer.

Key fact or strategy
Estimate/calculate or calculate/estimate to make a check on the answer reached.

Supplementary activities

Mental/oral follow-up Use Resource Sheet 4 to set up a game involving groups in the class. Display the resource sheet and assign each group several numbers. They can then determine how many of the numbers shown on Resource Sheet 4 have each of their numbers as one of a factor pair. For example, if a group are given 6 as one of their numbers, they should arrive at the following: 6 is a "pair factor" of 48, 60, 84, 96, 36, 72, 24, 18, 42, 66, 12, 90.

Homework Give the children more practice in finding the fractions of prices by allowing them to take home and complete Resource Sheet 6.

Development Resource Sheet 7 offers starting points for children to make up and solve their own money problems, both single- and multi-step. The items can be cut out and assigned different prices. The children's challenges can be worked on around the class.

ICT ideas The interactive whiteboard offers an ideal opportunity to model money problems. The Promethean whiteboard, for example, offers a range of prepared clipart including a sample set of notes and coins. These can be used for whole-class sessions covering money problems. It would be useful to prepare some clipart of objects, e.g. posters, CDs, etc. to which price labels can be attached. The children could then be asked to identify the cost of multiple items, to 'pay' for them using the clipart on the board and to identify 'change' from a shopping list of items, among many other possible activities.

The *Can Do Maths* series of CD-ROMs, published by Nelson Thornes, offers an easy way to introduce ICT resources to the classroom to support learning. Although many activities are intended for individual or paired work, each disc includes some opportunities for teachers to model mathematical ideas and methods and for children to explain their thinking.

Software programs of this type provide the opportunity to practise and reinforce basic number skills using a range of different context problems. They also offer a simple method of differentiating by task and by outcome as pupils' progress can be monitored and recorded.

The *10 minute series* of CD-ROMs, published by Granada Learning, serve a similar purpose.

Unit 2 Handling data

Term				Autumn 6	

Framework links

6	8	112–117	Handling data	Consolidate all previous work. Use language of probability, including events with equally likely outcomes. Present and interpret grouped discrete data on a bar chart.
		70–71	Using a calculator	Use prepared computer database to compare presentations of data. Find the mode and range of a set of data. Begin to find median and mean.

Setting the scene

In this unit the children will be able to work on and consolidate the vocabulary of probability. This is the most common everyday mathematical language. The children are given the chance to match theoretical probabilities against experimental outcomes. There are opportunities to work on the presentation of grouped data in bar charts. The interpretation and construction of these charts is addressed.
The latter half of the unit contains references to the uses of commercial computer databases for the presentation of data. This is followed by work on the modal average and the start of work on the median and the mean. In all cases the range is also explored. Such averages can be further explored by using databases.

Starting points

Throughout their school career, the children have worked on the important ideas relating to chance and probability together with a range of ways of handling data. They know some of the vocabulary of probability, what we mean by chance, and can rank events according to whether they are more or less likely. They have looked at, interpreted and created bar charts and bar line graphs. They know what the mode of a set of data denotes and they have created databases, at least on paper.

Checking progress

- All children should be able to discuss the likely outcome of events, explain why experimental results differ from theoretical predictions, interpret bar charts comprising grouped data and work with a computer database. They should be able to find and talk about the mode of a set of data.
- Children requiring additional support will need more oral work in discussing and explaining situations involving chance and probability. They need rehearsal in the key questions to ask oneself when interpreting or drawing up bar charts. Working with children at the computer may be necessary.
- Some children will have progressed further and will be keen to take their own experiments involving chance beyond two trials. They should be given more situations in which to determine probabilities and to determine how to present and interrogate information in a bar chart. They will be able to use databases to produce appropriate pictorial representations. They are beginning to look at the median and mean.

Lesson 1

Learning objectives

Mental/oral starter:
- Add any pair of two-digit numbers including crossing 100
- Subtract any pair of two-digit numbers including crossing 100

Main teaching activities:
- Use the language of probability
- Discuss the idea of events with two or more equally likely outcomes
- Experiment with events having two or more equally likely outcomes

Resources
Photocopies of Resource Sheet 8 (This could be printed up on thin card and the number squares should then be cut out in preparation for the lesson.), class-sized flashcards with the words listed in the vocabulary section below written on them (These should be made before the lesson.), photocopies of General Resource Sheet A (Spinner 1 only is required – enough for one spinner per pair of children should be printed on thin card.), scissors to cut the spinners out, a spent match for each spinner, a resource box containing dice, coins or replica coins, one or two packs of playing cards

Vocabulary
Fair, unfair, likely, unlikely, likelihood, equally likely, certain, uncertain, probable, possible, impossible, chance, good chance, poor chance, no chance, equal chance, even chance, fifty-fifty chance, risk, biased, random

MENTAL/ORAL STARTER

Place all the number cards made up from Resource Sheet 8 into an open small box. Shake the numbers around. Move about the class giving individual children the chance to take out two numbers at random. They should say the numbers aloud, sum them and then say the difference between them. Return to the front of the class. Take out more pairs of numbers and write them on the board. Ask the children to call out the sum and the difference.

MAIN ACTIVITY

Whole class, pairs, small groups

Hold up each of the flashcards in turn and give the children an instance of its use. Here are some examples.

Duncan kept on throwing 5s on the dice because the dice was **unfair**.

The players had the same number of cards each to make the game **fair**.

It is **likely** that there will be clouds in the sky tomorrow.

It is **unlikely** that I shall win the lottery.

The **likelihood** of me being an Oscar winner is low.

If I toss a coin heads and tails are **equally likely**.

It is **certain** that it will get dark tonight.

It is **uncertain** whether the USA will win most medals in the next Olympics.

It is **probable** that it will rain somewhere in Britain next week.

It is **possible** that someone in the class will be a teacher when they grow up.

It is **impossible** that I shall grow younger each day.

You have a **chance** of becoming famous.

You have a **good chance** of learning some maths.

You have a **poor chance** of becoming world chess champion.

There is **no chance** that Christmas Day will change from 25 December.

When a dice is thrown there is an **equal chance** that each of the numbers will come up.

When a coin is tossed there is an **even chance** of it showing heads or tails.

If two tickets remain and one is a prize ticket, we have a **fifty-fifty chance** of winning.

There is a **risk** that we shall not win when we enter a raffle.

A **biased** dice will show one or more numbers more than others when it is thrown many times.

I found a **random** number by closing my eyes and pointing at a page of the telephone book.

Show the children a spinner (from General Resource Sheet A). Ask what the chances are of spinning a 1, then a 2, a 3, and so on. The children should understand that theoretically there is an even chance (the same chance) of each number coming up. Organise the children into pairs to make up their spinners. Each pair then take turns to spin the spinner, 20 times altogether, and record the number that comes up each time.

■ **Support**

Remind the children that there are measures they can take to make the performance of their spinner fair. They should place the spinner on the same surface to spin each time, and not disturb its spin. Ask them again to predict what the outcome of their 20 spins will be. (Theoretically each number should come up 20 ÷ 6 times, that is about 3 or 4 times.)

■ **Challenge**

Ask the children to discuss what would happen if the spinner had five or eight sides, or if one side was left blank and did not count. How would these changes affect how often each number has a chance of coming up?

PLENARY

Obtain the spinner results from each pair of children and collate them all together in a chart, numbered 1–6. Discuss the distribution over the whole class. Did any pair have lots of the same number or numbers? Discuss what would be a fair outcome.

In the light of their experience, talk about the probability of getting the following when spinning the spinner:

- a 5
- an even number
- a zero
- a number more than 3.

Draw a probability scale on the board and explain what it means to the children. Here is a suggested scale.

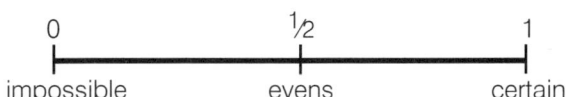

Discuss where on the scale the probabilities above might come.

Key fact or strategy
A 50 per cent chance, evens, even chance or fifty-fifty chance is when an outcome is as likely as not and is, therefore, placed in the middle of a probability scale.

Lesson 2

Learning objectives

Mental/oral starter:
- Derive the sum of two numbers
- Derive the difference between two numbers

Main teaching activities:
- Use the language of probability
- Discuss further events with equally likely outcomes
- Experiment with events having two or more equally likely outcomes

Resources
Three-digit number cards for the mental/oral starter (These cards should be made prior to the lesson. There are some starter numbers on Resource Sheet 9. General Resource Sheet F provides a blank grid, of the same size, on which you can enter more numbers.), a small opaque fabric "feely" bag that opens at one end, 4 large beads or blocks of different colours, photocopies of Resource Sheet 10, a 2p coin for each pair of children

Vocabulary
Fair, unfair, likely, unlikely, likelihood, equally likely, certain, uncertain, probable, possible, impossible, chance, good chance, poor chance, no chance, equal chance, even chance, fifty-fifty chance, risk, biased, random

MENTAL/ORAL STARTER

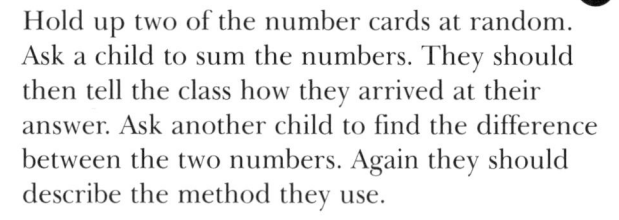

Hold up two of the number cards at random. Ask a child to sum the numbers. They should then tell the class how they arrived at their answer. Ask another child to find the difference between the two numbers. Again they should describe the method they use.

Take up another pair of numbers at random and invite individual children to sum them and find the difference. Do this several times. Check whether some of the children are using different methods to solve the problems. Confirm the usefulness of approximation, rounding and estimation in problem solving.

MAIN ACTIVITY

Whole class, pairs

Take up the "feely" bag and place two blocks inside, in full view of the children so that they can see there is one each of two different colours, for example, red and blue. Ask the children:

What is the chance of taking a red block or a blue block from the bag?

Establish that each colour has an equal chance. Either red or blue is equally likely so there are two equally likely outcomes. Try with two other colours of blocks, and a third time with a new combination.

Add a third block to the bag. The children should note that each colour still has a similar chance, that is an equal chance, of being pulled from the bag. This time there are three possible outcomes. When a fourth block is added to the bag the chance is still equal for each colour, and there are four possible outcomes.

Discuss with the children some events that have two equally likely outcomes in everyday life, for example, a new baby can be a boy or a girl, a coin when tossed comes up heads or tails.

Give each pair of children a coin and each child a copy of Resource Sheet 10. Ask the children each to make a tally of 30 tosses of their coin and record the outcomes in the Trial 1 columns of their resource sheet.

■ Support
Check that the children are taking turns to toss the coin and then marking in the outcomes as a stroke or tick in the appropriate columns on the resource sheet. Ask them questions to provoke further thinking.

What outcomes do you expect?

Is the chance of getting heads the same each time you toss the coin?

■ Challenge
Ask the children to work out all the possible outcomes if they were given two coins.

Call the class together and collate results. Then let the pairs of children try again for 30 more tosses of the coin. Collate the results again and discuss them with the children. Are they close to evens? Do the results get more like the theoretical results, the more times the coin is tossed?

> **Key fact or strategy**
> The more times an event occurs the greater the likelihood that the outcomes will approach theoretical predictions regarding outcomes.

PLENARY

In this lesson the children are looking again at equally likely outcomes. In everyday life, the idea of luck often affects some of us. We tend to think that if some event has not happened for a while it is bound to happen soon. It is important to assure the children that dice, beads, spinners, coins, even lottery balls do not have memories.

> **Learning objectives**
> *Mental/oral starter:*
> • Derive sums and differences between three-digit numbers
> *Main teaching activities:*
> • Extract and interpret data from bar charts showing grouped discrete data
>
> **Resources**
> Photocopies of Resource Sheet 11, an OHT of Resource Sheet 11
>
> **Vocabulary**
> Bar chart, data, discrete, grouped

MENTAL/ORAL STARTER

Write digits on the board like this:
0 1 2 3 4 5 6 7 8 9.

Ask a child to make up a three-digit number (they can choose a digit more than once). Write the number on the board. Ask another child to make up a number. The numbers may be: 422 and 583.

Work through how these numbers can be summed and how the difference between them can be found. In the example given, for the addition, we may say:

422 is 420 + 2 and 583 is 580 + 3

580 + 420 = 1000

3 + 2 = 5

1000 + 5 = 1005.

To find the difference, we can take 400 from 500 and 22 from 83 and then sum the outcomes, that is 100 + 61 = 161.

Ask the children for other methods of working out the addition and subtraction.

Return to the digit list and repeat the exercise.

MAIN ACTIVITY

Whole class, individuals, small groups

Ask the children what a bar chart is. Check that they know that it is a graph where the information is shown in columns or bars. Remind the children of the following facts about bar charts.

• Bar charts can be constructed only after all the data has been collected.
• Bar charts are a step towards bar line graphs, and it is the height of the bar that is crucial.
• The bars on a chart all have the same width.

Draw bar charts on the board, as shown here.

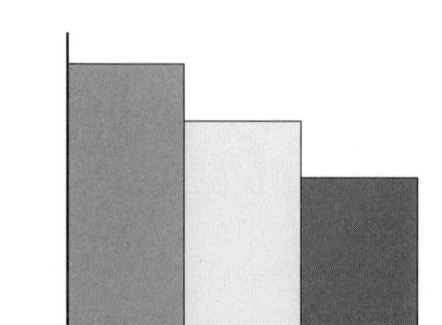

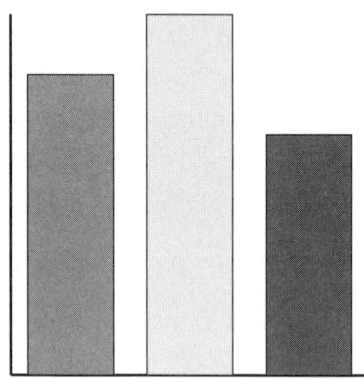

Point out to the children that the bars on a bar chart can be vertical or horizontal, and need not touch one another. Unless a bar chart is properly labelled, it tells us nothing.

Show the OHT of Resource Sheet 11. Read through the challenges and discuss how to find the answers. Ask some more oral challenges:

Which rainfall range occurred at more places, 7–8 cm or 3–4 cm?

Thirty locations reported 5–6 cm of rain. Another 30 all reported the same rainfall range, what was it?

Give each child a copy of Resource Sheet 11 and ask them to complete it.

■ **Support**
Work through the challenges one by one with the children.

■ **Challenge**
Ask the children to offer help and guidance to children who have not yet completed the task.

PLENARY

Draw this bar chart on the board.

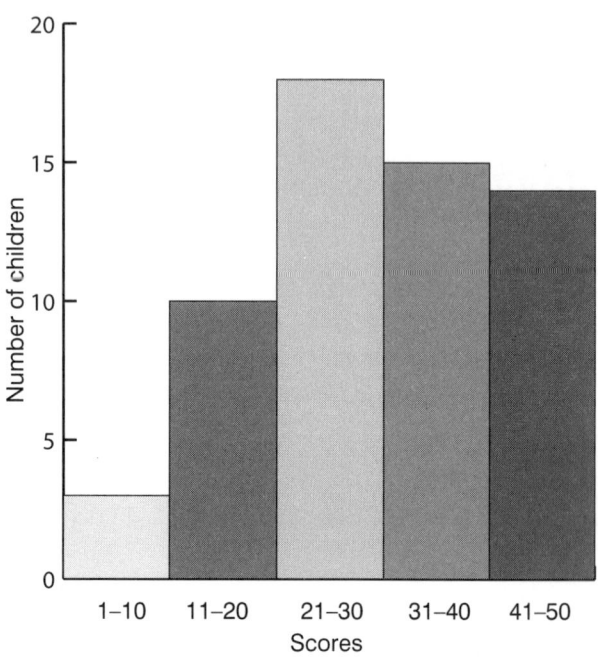

Scores in a times table test taken by two classes

Talk about what it shows. With the children's help, solve a number of challenges. Here are some suggestions.

How many children scored 11–20, 31–40?

What was the most/least common score range?

Fifteen children were in the same score range. What was it?

Key fact or strategy
An understanding of the key attributes of bar charts listed in the introduction to the lesson is essential.

Lesson 4

Learning objectives
Mental/oral starter:
- Recall multiplication facts in the 2, 4 and 8 times tables

Main teaching activities:
- Present and interpret grouped discrete data on a bar chart

Resources
Photocopies of Resource Sheet 12

Vocabulary
Bar chart, data, discrete, grouped

MENTAL/ORAL STARTER

In quick-fire succession, ask the children to give you products at random in the 2, 4 and 8 times tables, for example, call out:

$9 \times 2 \quad 3 \times 4$
$5 \times 8 \quad 7 \times 8$
$9 \times 4 \quad 7 \times 2$

When all the products have been asked for at least twice, write the products on the board in lists so that they line up. Here is how to begin:

$1 \times 2 = 2$
$2 \times 2 = 4 \qquad 1 \times 4 = 4$
$3 \times 2 = 6$
$4 \times 2 = 8 \qquad 2 \times 4 = 8 \qquad 1 \times 8 = 8$
$5 \times 2 = 10$
$6 \times 2 = 12 \qquad 3 \times 4 = 12$

Discuss the transferability across the tables: the fact that, for example, 2×4 gives a product the same as 4×2 and that 2×2 is 4 and $2 \times 2 \times 2$ (2×4) is 8.

MAIN ACTIVITY

Whole class, individuals

Talk to the children about the difference between discrete data (where every item stands alone and cannot be joined to the next, for points in between have no meaning) and data, such as that involving time, which we call continuous.

Write on the board the following data relating to the amount of time some children spent in doing homework one day. The data has already been grouped.

Number of children	Time spent (minutes)
4	1–15
7	16–30
10	31–45
12	46–60
3	61–75

Draw a bar chart while the children look on. The finished chart should look like this.

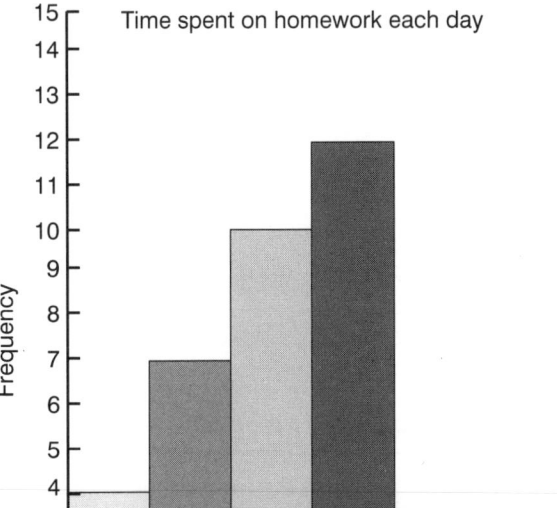

Remind the children that the groupings for the data are all of the same size and do not overlap.

Give out copies of Resource Sheet 12. Talk through the task and then ask each child to complete the chart by grouping the data appropriately.

■ Support
Sit with the children and, as a group, help them to decide on the groupings for the data, before measuring up their axes ready for the bars.

■ Challenge
The children can compile three questions that can be answered by consulting their bar chart. They can also exchange charts with other children and compare the results.

PLENARY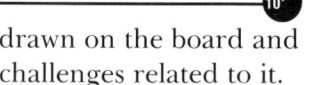

Return to the bar chart drawn on the board and offer the children some challenges related to it. Here are some examples.

How many children spent 30 minutes or less on their homework?

What was the time range that the biggest group of children spent on homework?

What is the longest time anyone could have spent on homework?

How many children supplied these data?

Key fact or strategy

Carefully inspect the data range to make groupings that reveal most about the data and make it easy to present the information on the page.

Lesson 5

Learning objectives
Mental/oral starter:
- Recall multiplication and division facts to 10 × 10

Main teaching activities:
- Use a computer database to compare pictorial representations

Resources
Computer, database software, some commercially produced data sets (Examples can be found in the Nelson Thornes Primary ICT Granada Toolkit and in the National Numeracy Strategy *Using ICT to support mathematics in Primary Schools* pack.), photocopies of Resource Sheet 13, books and other sources of information about planets in the solar system

Vocabulary
Data, database, software, sets, line graphs, bars, charts

MENTAL/ORAL STARTER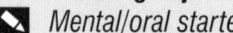

Focus on the 3, 6 and 9 times tables. Start by giving some quick-fire multiplications from these tables. Invite the children to tell you just the products from each table. Write these in columns on the board.

3x	6x	9x
3	6	9
6	12	18
9	18	27
12	24	36
15	30	45
18	36	54
21	42	63
24	48	72
27	54	81
30	60	90

Ask the children to tell you about the connections that they can see between the columns of products.

Can you see a way of finding the products of the 6 times table from the 3 and the 9 times tables?

MAIN ACTIVITY

Whole class, small groups

The organisation and sequencing of this lesson depends upon the availability of computers. The intention is to allow the children to explore given data sets by using a database and with a view to presenting those data in different ways. You could, for example, use a database to sort numbers, data gathered using sensors relating to temperature, sound or other environmental change or data about animal life. Once the children have presented the data, they should make comparisons. They need to use appropriate representations, for example, line graphs should not be employed with discrete data. Resource Sheet 13 is provided so that some children can work away from the computer. It supplies some starter information about the planets. This can be the basis for a database that the children can research further by using classroom resources. The next lesson is like this one and you may choose to blend the two or even have a block of time for using computer databases.

■ **Support**
Pairs of children work at the computer, with appropriate support.

■ **Challenge**
The children can research some data further and use their findings in a database.

PLENARY

Depending on the progress of different groups, have at least one interim discussion and display examples of representations. Discuss the appropriateness or otherwise of different presentations.

> **Key fact or strategy**
> Database packages assist in the sorting and pictorial representation of data.

Lesson 6

Learning objectives
Mental/oral starter:
- Convert between km, m, cm and mm

Main teaching activities:
- Use a computer database to compare pictorial representations

Resources
Computer, database software, some commercially produced data sets, photocopies of Resource Sheet 13

Vocabulary
Data, database, software, sets, line graphs, bars, charts, metric measures

MENTAL/ORAL STARTER

Write km, m, cm and mm on the board and ask what they stand for. Ask what the relationship is between each of these metric measures of length. Use the relationships to pose questions.

How many millimetres in a metre?

How many centimetres in a kilometre?

Give some measures and ask for conversions. Here are some examples.

Metric measure of length

256 cm	How many metres and centimetres?
45 mm	How many centimetres?
6700 mm	How many metres and centimetres?
1.5 km	How many metres?
0.25 km	How many metres and centimetres?

MAIN ACTIVITY

Whole class, small groups

As in the previous lesson, access to computers or a mixture of computer and desk-based work is required. Allow the children to continue their exploration of databases and representations of provided data. Resource Sheet 13 can be used for preparatory work and/or for inputting to a database.

■ **Support**
The children should work in small groups at the computer, with appropriate support.

■ **Challenge**
The children should collect some new data and use it in a database.

PLENARY

Once again give the plenary session over to reviewing what has been achieved so far. Continue to review the appropriateness and usefulness of different ways of presenting data.

> **Key fact or strategy**
> Database packages assist in the sorting and pictorial representation of data.

Lesson 7

Learning objectives
Mental/oral starter:
- Convert between km, m, cm and mm

Main teaching activities:
- Find the mode and range of a set of data
- Begin to find median

Resources
Photocopies of Resource Sheet 14

Vocabulary
Average, mode, range, median

MENTAL/ORAL STARTER

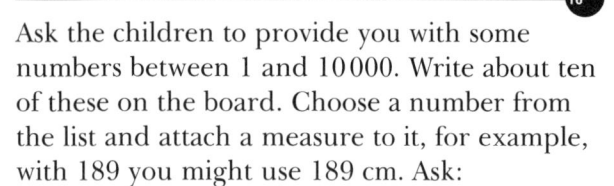

Ask the children to provide you with some numbers between 1 and 10 000. Write about ten of these on the board. Choose a number from the list and attach a measure to it, for example, with 189 you might use 189 cm. Ask:

How many metres?

How many millimetres?

Do this for each of the given numbers.

MAIN ACTIVITY

Whole class, pairs

Use these timings of phone calls to revise mode and range.

Phone calls to friends

	Minutes
Esme	6
Johan	8
Alex	4
Robin	3
Raekha	2
Alex	8
Julia	5
Dino	5
Alex	2
Esme	16
Dino	8

Give out Resource Sheet 14 and ask the children to work in pairs on Section A. When this is completed, work through both questions by asking different pairs to guide the class.

Use the numbers shown here to introduce the idea of median.

13   17   14   13   18   19   13   14   19

When you feel that the class is ready, ask the pairs to tackle Section B.

■ **Support**
The children work through only the first question in Section A of Resource Sheet 14.

■ **Challenge**
The children can use the data in Section A in a computer database.

PLENARY

Work through Section B of Resource Sheet 14. Use this as an opportunity to review range, mode and median.

> **Key fact or strategy**
> There are several ways to consider average.

Lesson 8

> **Learning objectives**
> *Mental/oral starter:*
> - Multiply mentally any two-digit number by a one-digit number
>
> *Main teaching activities:*
> - Find the mode and range of a set of data
> - Begin to find median and mean
>
> **Resources**
> Photocopies of Resource Sheet 15, an OHT of Resource Sheet 15
>
> **Vocabulary**
> Average, mode, median, mean, range, digit

MENTAL/ORAL STARTER

Ask the children for some two-digit numbers. Use, say, five of the suggestions. Ask the children to multiply the chosen numbers by a single-digit number that you choose. Discuss the strategies employed.

MAIN ACTIVITY

Whole class, pairs

Use the figures shown here to review range, mode and median.

3, 9, 8, 8, 8, 4, 5, 3, 6

range is 6
mode is 8
median is 6

Total = 54 so mean is $54/9 = 6$

Use the same figures to introduce the idea of mean average. When the children have grasped the concepts, give out Resource Sheet 15. The children work in pairs to answer the questions.

■ Support

Give the children some more sets of simple figures for them to work out the mean.

■ Challenge

The children can work with a partner to explain why averages might be different.

PLENARY

Use the OHT that you have made of Resource Sheet 15 to stimulate different pairs to talk through range, mode, median and mean. Take the opportunity to revise how we determine each of the averages.

> **Key fact or strategy**
> There are three ways we should know of determining an average.

Supplementary activities

Mental/oral follow-up

Create a bank of cards with two-digit numbers on them and invite the children to take "lucky dips" of pairs to total. Use the same cards to rehearse multiplication by a single-digit number. A similar approach can be used for the addition and subtraction of three-digit numbers. Give different times tables to pairs to explore for patterns. Get pairs to write up and share with the class all that they discover. Obtain reference books that contain measurements and use these to do conversion work.

Homework

Give the children a copy of Resource Sheet 16 and ask them to play by rolling a dice at home. They should roll the dice 30 times and record the numbers that came up. They can write a short comment about their results. If they bring the completed sheets into school, the results can be collated to compile probability results for the class. Further discussions can be had, for example, about the following:

- If a dice is thrown twice and the scores are summed, what is the range of scores?
- If you play a game where there are two players, each throwing the dice twice, and player 1 wins the turn if the score is less than 6, and player 2 wins the turn if the score is 6 or more, is the game fair?

A grid of possible scores is shown here.

Chart of possible outcomes when two dice throws are summed

+	1	2	3	4	5	6
1	2	3	4	5	6	7
2	3	4	5	6	7	8
3	4	5	6	7	8	9
4	5	6	7	8	9	10
5	6	7	8	9	10	11
6	7	8	9	10	11	12

Development

Probability: Organise the children into pairs to talk about and try to complete the work on Resource Sheet 17. (The discussion points on this resource sheet are quite complex and children needing support may benefit from having coins, dice and cards to work with.)
The outcomes in "A" are: head/tail; odd/even; red card/black card.
When the children have mastered the concept of equally likely outcomes they will be ready to tackle the work on Resource Sheet 18.

ICT ideas

Maths Explorer: Data Handling (Granada Learning) can be used to introduce the concept of probability. On entering the program, pupils can view facts and general information about probability and chance. They can then move to different investigations with up to three levels of difficulty, including calculating the probability of certain numbers being spun on a wheel or plotting the probability of certain events on a number line.

Database packages might be used in a whole-class setting during mathematics lessons as much time can be wasted in familiarising children with the creation of the database structure. You might therefore establish a central database using data collected from the children's 'paper databases'. Children could then pool their findings into a single common database. According to their ICT ability, children should then search the data and display the results as charts. A text commentary might also be added for a classroom display.

Granada Database (part of the 'Granada Toolkit') is a fully featured data-handling package, where children can collect and store information. The package includes a range of graphing facilities including bar charts and bar line graphs. Other packages include Information *Workshop* (BlackCat), *Junior ViewPoint* (Logotron) and *Textease Database* (Textease).

Unit 3   Measures problems, including time

Term Autumn 8-10

Framework links

8–10	15	102–111	Shape and space	Consolidate all previous work. Classify quadrilaterals using side/angle properties. Read and plot co-ordinates in all four quadrants. Recognise where a shape will be after two translations.
		76–81	Reasoning about shapes	Solve shape puzzles. Explain methods and reasoning orally and in writing. Calculate perimeter of rectangles and simple compound shapes.
		86–101	Measures, including problems	Use, read and write standard metric units of length, abbreviations and relationships. Convert larger to smaller units of length and vice versa. Know mile and km equivalents. Appreciate different times around the world. Suggest suitable units/equipment to estimate or measure length. Record estimates/measurements from scales to suitable degree of accuracy. Use all four operations to solve measurement word problems, including time. Choose appropriate operations/calculation methods. Explain working.

Setting the scene	In this unit the children have another opportunity to work on word problems involving measures. We start with the measurement of length because this is the measurement that we use so much in everyday life. The focus is on the use of metric units (km, m and cm) for measuring length. There is also a reference to the millimetre and to some imperial measures (the inch, yard and mile) in the Homework and Development sections. This unit also includes work on time taken and on interpreting timetables.
Starting points	During the previous years of their primary schooling the children will have had prodigious experience in solving problems involving length and time. They will have mastered the idea that the key to achieving the correct answer is to carefully choose the operations required to arrive at a solution. They should have had opportunities to talk about how they worked out solutions. The children should also understand that there is often more than one appropriate method for solving a problem. They should have met timetables and be able to begin to interpret them.
Checking progress	■ All children should be able to work with standard units of length including km, m, cm, mm and with inches, yards and miles, when necessary. They should be able to extract information from simple timetables. ■ Children requiring additional support will need to be talked through the standard units we use and how we convert one to the other. They will need help in deciding on a strategy for solving each problem. Clues about how to approach reading a table (by using information that is shown vertically and horizontally) would be helpful. ■ Some children will have progressed further and will be adept at solving multi-step problems using standard measures of length and measures of time. They will be able to invent challenges for their classmates.

Lesson 1

Learning objectives
Mental/oral starter:
- Order fractions

Main teaching activities:
- Use addition, subtraction, multiplication and division to solve measures problems involving length
- Choose appropriate operations
- Explain how they worked them out

Resources
At least three balls of string, rope or twine, of different thickness (These should be collected beforehand for use in the introduction to the lesson.), photocopies of Resource Sheet 19

Vocabulary
Fraction, rank order, metre, centimetre, m, cm, method, calculation, operation, addition, subtraction, multiplication, division

MENTAL/ORAL STARTER

Write up a series of fractions on the board. Here are some suggested fractions to start with.

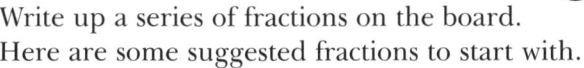

Ask the children which they think is the smallest. Mark this in some way, for example, as "f1". Ask for the next smallest fraction, and so on, until all the fractions are marked. Discuss with the children how they can determine that their ranking is correct.

Write another collection of fractions on the board and play the game again. Repeat the activity several times.

MAIN ACTIVITY

Whole class, individuals, small groups

Set out the balls of string and devise some problems related to them that can be worked through as examples. Point to one of the balls and say:

Let us pretend there are 23 metres of string on this ball. If I cut 7.5 metres off, how much is left on the ball?

If I take 4 lengths of 3 metres each from the whole ball, how much will I cut off?

These examples can be written up on the board and worked through with the children.

Take up other balls of string in turn and work through a couple of challenges with each of them.

Give out copies of Resource Sheet 19.

■ Support
Help the children to determine which operation they will use, before they tackle each problem.

■ Challenge
The children can form into groups and examine each other's methods and answers, in readiness for the plenary session.

PLENARY

Ask individual children in turn to share how they worked out the answers to the problems on the resource sheet. List on the board the strategies that the children have used.

> **Key fact or strategy**
> Ensure that measurements are in similar units before operating on them.

Lesson 2

Learning objectives

Mental/oral starter:
- Add/subtract any pair of two-digit numbers

Main teaching activities:
- Use addition, subtraction, multiplication and division to solve measures problems involving length
- Choose appropriate operations
- Explain how they worked them out
- Use calculators to check, devise and solve problems

Resources
Four books from the class library (These should be selected beforehand to use in the mental/oral starter.), photocopies of Resource Sheet 20, calculators (enough for one per pair)

Vocabulary
Fraction, rank order, kilometre, metre, centimetre, km, m, cm, method, calculation, operation, addition, subtraction, multiplication, division

MENTAL/ORAL STARTER

Hand out the four library books to four children in the class. Ask them in turn to open their book anywhere to reveal a two-digit page number, then close the book and do the same again. Write each pair of numbers on the board, until there are four pairs.

In quick-fire succession, ask the children to sum and find the difference between each pair of numbers in turn.

Ask the children who are holding the books to pass them on to someone else in the class. Play the game, in this way, several times.

MAIN ACTIVITY

Whole class, individuals, pairs

Remind the children of the relationship between a kilometre, a metre and a centimetre.

Give a copy of Resource Sheet 20 to each child. Invite the children to do the three sections as follows:

- A – individually
- B – talked through with a partner
- C – worked through with a partner.
  (The children draw a rough sketch of the multi-sports trail and tie in the arithmetic problems. They use a calculator to help them.)

▪ Support
Sit with children who are having difficulty with Section A. Draw a rough trail of the multi-sport challenge so that they can see which distances are relevant to the actual calculation they are doing. Allow the children access to calculators to check their work.

▪ Challenge
The children who readily complete Sections A and B can work up a set of challenges for their classmates.

PLENARY

Confirm the answers and some of the methods used for solving the problems in Section A. If there is time, present to the class some of the children's work from Section C. Set this work aside for checking, so that it can be added to a challenge bank for the development section at the end of the unit.

> **Key fact or strategy**
> A calculator can help when we are checking or deriving arithmetic problems.

Lesson 3

Learning objectives
Mental/oral starter:
- Add/subtract any pair of two-digit numbers

Main teaching activities:
- Use addition, subtraction, multiplication and division to solve time problems
- Choose appropriate operations
- Explain how they worked them out

Resources
Photocopy General Resource Sheet G onto thin card (The cards should be cut out ready for use in the mental/oral starter.), photocopies of Resource Sheet 21

Vocabulary
Digit, sum, difference, time, minute, hour, method, calculation, operation, addition, subtraction, multiplication, division

MENTAL/ORAL STARTER

Shuffle the digit cards made up for the lesson. Take the top two from the pile and hold them up to make a two-digit number. Take the next two and make a second two-digit number. Ask the children to sum these numbers and find the difference between them.

Repeat this process until the pile of digit cards is exhausted. Take up the used cards and shuffle them before beginning again.

MAIN ACTIVITY
Whole class, individuals, pairs

Ask the children the key questions about our measurement of time to remind them of units and their relationships, in particular, that there are 60 minutes in an hour.

Take up the Resource Sheet 21 and write a copy of the table on the board. Work through the table with the children's help. Write in the answers. When the table is complete, wipe it off the board.

Give a copy of Resource Sheet 21 to each child. The children should complete Section A individually and then work on Section B with a partner.

■ Support
As completion of the chart has been worked through as a class activity, the children should be able to tackle Section A individually. They should work as a group to try to solve Section B.

■ Challenge
The children can extend the table for ever larger rugs. Here are some starter figures for them: 20 kg, 22.5 kg, 35 kg, 60 kg.

PLENARY

Go through the resource sheet once more. Check the strategies that individual children used to solve the problems.

> **Key fact or strategy**
> Work in minutes before conversion to hours and minutes.

Lesson 4

Learning objectives

Mental/oral starter:
- Convert between km, m, cm, and mm and vice versa

Main teaching activities:
- Use addition, subtraction, multiplication and division to solve time problems
- Choose appropriate operations
- Explain how they worked them out

Resources
Photocopy Resource Sheet 22 onto thin card (It would be useful to double the size of the cards. Cut out the individual cards ready for the mental/oral starter.), a "washing line" and pegs (The washing line should stretch across the classroom in front of the children. Clip the pegs along its length.), an OHT of Resource Sheet 23, photocopies of Resource Sheet 23, pocket train timetables (These should be collected beforehand from the local station.)

Vocabulary
km, m, cm, mm, time, minute, hour, method, calculation, operation, addition, subtraction, multiplication, division

MENTAL/ORAL STARTER

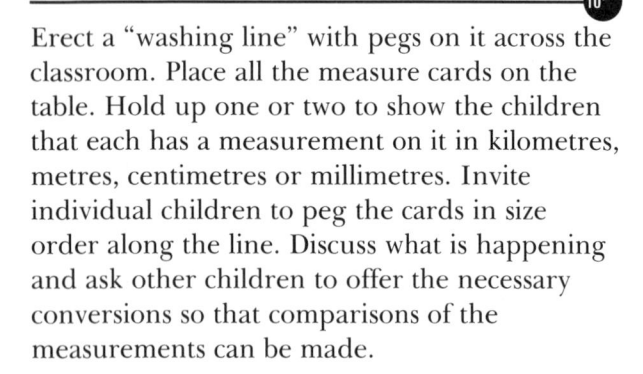

Erect a "washing line" with pegs on it across the classroom. Place all the measure cards on the table. Hold up one or two to show the children that each has a measurement on it in kilometres, metres, centimetres or millimetres. Invite individual children to peg the cards in size order along the line. Discuss what is happening and ask other children to offer the necessary conversions so that comparisons of the measurements can be made.

MAIN ACTIVITY

Whole class, pairs

Discuss why it is that we need timetables and ask the children key questions to test their understanding.

What does a timetable tell us?

What are the two sets of information presented on a timetable?

Why is it called a timetable?

Display the OHT of Resource Sheet 23 so that all the children can see it clearly. Talk through what it presents. Show the inward and outward journey, the departure times and indicate where the arrival and departure times differ. Answer any questions that the children may have about the interpretation of the timetable.

Give each pair of children a copy of Resource Sheet 23. They should work on the challenges together and then each make a record of the work they have done in their workbooks.

Support
Help the children who find the timetable too complex to look at it a section at a time. They can work out the time taken from each station to the next. If these are written on a group chart of the journey, they will then find it easier to solve the problems.

Challenge
Allow the children to look together at a real pocket timetable and see if they can interpret it.

PLENARY

Show again the OHT of Resource Sheet 23. Take each challenge in turn and ask the children how they worked it out. Compare the methods the children have used.

> **Key fact or strategy**
>
> To read a timetable we need to look at the information that is set across and down the table.

Supplementary activities

Mental/oral follow-up   Use the digit cards made up from General Resource Sheet G. Ask two children to stand at the front and take turns to select two cards each. These can be held aloft while the rest of the class work out the sum of the two two-digit numbers and the difference between them.

Use the cards made up from Resource Sheet 22. Hold up two at a time and ask the children which is the longer or which is the shorter. Hold up each measurement card in turn and challenge a child to convert it, for example, 1.5 metres in centimetres is 1500.

Homework   Resource Sheet 24 can be given to the children to work on at home.

Development   Use the work on the multi-sport challenge that the children did in Lesson 2 as a starting point to stimulate groups to set similar problem-solving challenges for each other.

Take some of the pocket timetables collected from your local station and give the children challenges relating to them. The questions could include the following:

How long does it take to get from ... to ...?
What is the quickest route from ... to ...?
What is the difference in travel times when comparing a through train and a stopping train on the same route?

ICT ideas   *Cars – Maths in Motion* (Cambridgeshire Software House) is a simulation program that is based on a whole season of Formula 1 motor racing. The program could form part of a whole Maths Week as it incorporates so many different mathematical concepts. Groups can be allocated to teams who have to set up their 'car' by:

- categorising the circuit plans – by measuring angles and using scale drawings
- calculating race distance – in kilometres
- determining safe speeds and entering race speeds – in kilometres per hour.

The program includes many other problem-solving activities incorporating all of the measures, including time, that the children will have covered in previous lessons.

Unit 4 "Real-life" problems

Term				Autumn 11	
Framework links					
5	1	40–47 48–51	Mental calculation strategies (+ and −)	Consolidate all previous work. Use related facts and doubling or halving, for example, halve an even number, double the other; multiply by 25, by × 100, then ÷ by 4. Approximate first.	
		82–85	Pencil and paper procedures (× and ÷)	If appropriate; use informal pencil and paper methods to support, record or explain × and ÷. Extend written methods to column + and − numbers involving decimals.	
		70–75	Money and "real-life" problems Making decisions and checking results, including using a calculator	Use all four operations to solve money or "real-life" word problems. Choose appropriate operations/calculation methods. Explain working.	

Setting the scene In solving problems involving numbers or quantities, it is often the case that, whilst children can carry through a computation correctly, they mistake the operation/s that are involved. In this unit a variety of problems is offered which involve the children in choosing the correct operations and then obtaining the solution.

Starting points The children have had progressive engagement with computation methods over the years. They should be skilful at a range of pencil and paper methods, both formal and informal. They have also had considerable experience in the solving of "real-life" problems.

Checking progress
- All children should know at least one way of carrying out each of the four operations.
- Children requiring additional support will need some support in reviewing their knowledge of the variety of terms for operations.
- Some children will have progressed further and find that they have an almost instinctive feel for the right operation and/or the sequencing of operations. Some children may be able to offer alternative strategies or techniques for problem solution.

Lesson 1

Learning objectives
Mental/oral starter:
- Count on/back in steps of 25

Main teaching activities:
- Use all four operations to solve "real-life" problems
- Choose appropriate operations/calculation methods
- Explain working

Resources
Calculators, photocopies of Resource Sheet 25

Vocabulary
Addition, subtraction, multiplication, division, problem, solve, solution

MENTAL/ORAL STARTER

Start with a warm-up of counting on in 10s from 0, then in 5s. Ask the children to count on from 0 in 25s.

How far can you go?

Give the children something other than 0 to start from, say 5. Use 0.25 as a starting point. Finish by counting back from 100 to 0 in 25s then from 10 to 0 in 2.5s and finally from 1 to 0 in 0.25s.

MAIN ACTIVITY

Whole class, pairs

Ask the children what the four operations are. Tell the class:

In this lesson you are going to have to decide which operations you need to use to solve some problems.

Give out Resource Sheet 25 to pairs of children. Tell them that they can use a calculator to check their solutions when they have done the problems.

■ Support
Work through the first problem with the children.

■ Challenge
The children can make a chart of the figures relating to stocks of plates in question 3 on Resource Sheet 25.

PLENARY

Go through the resource sheet problem by problem, and in each case ask:

What operation or operations do you need for this one?

How did you decide?

What is the solution?

Collect in the work for checking.

Key fact or strategy
To determine the required operation or operations it is important to read carefully and make use of the knowledge of different terms for the same operation.

Lesson 2

Learning objectives
Mental/oral starter:
- Mentally multiply any two-digit number to 50 by a one-digit number

Main teaching activities:
- Use all four operations to solve "real-life" problems
- Choose appropriate operations/calculation methods
- Explain working

Resources
Calculators, photocopies of Resource Sheet 26, a road map of the area in which your school is situated (Miles or kilometres should be marked on the roads.)

Vocabulary
Addition, subtraction, multiplication, division, problem, solve, solution

MENTAL/ORAL STARTER

Use the road map of the area to choose some places that are more than 10 miles (or kilometres) away from the school. Tell the children that you know a delivery person who has to deliver motor parts in your area. Some days they may have to travel back and forth 2, 3, 4 and up to 9 times. Choose the number of deliveries to a place and ask the children to give you the total distance covered by multiplying mentally the number of journeys by the distance.

MAIN ACTIVITY

Whole class, pairs

Tell the class:

As in the last lesson, you are going to have to decide which operations you need to solve some problems.

Give out Resource Sheet 26 to pairs of children. Tell them that they can use a calculator to check their solutions when they have done the problems.

■ Support
Go over one of the problems on the resource sheet with the children.

■ Challenge
The children can invent a similar problem by developing one of the ideas on the resource sheet.

PLENARY

Go through the resource sheet problem by problem, and in each case ask:

What operation or operations do you need for this one?

How did you decide?

What is the solution?

Collect in the work for checking.

> **Key fact or strategy**
> Vocabulary and the interpretation of a range of terms for the same operation continue to be of central importance.

Supplementary activities

Mental/oral follow-up

Do lots of counting on and back in 5s, 10s, 20s, 25s, 50s and 100s. Ask the children to prepare two-digit by one-digit questions to challenge others in the class. Use these as a data bank for five or ten minute sessions on mental multiplication.

Homework

Ask the children to question adults at home about the operations that they use in a typical week for such things as shopping, DIY, driving, checking bills, and so on.

Development

Ask the children to take one or more of the settings offered in Resource Sheets 25 and 26 and ask them to see if they can create any new problems. They should check these out for the operations needed, and whether the vocabulary is appropriate. They should have solutions. Then some or all of these problems could be used as extension opportunities for individuals or groups, as appropriate.

ICT ideas

Lifeskills Time and Money (Learning and Teaching Scotland) offers a range of stimulating activities set within a townscape where children are encouraged to learn by solving puzzles and managing everyday situations. The teacher can customise the content of this package to meet the needs of individual ability levels.

GridClub, the online project for 7–11 year olds, at http://www.gridclub.com contains many appropriate interactive games and puzzles.

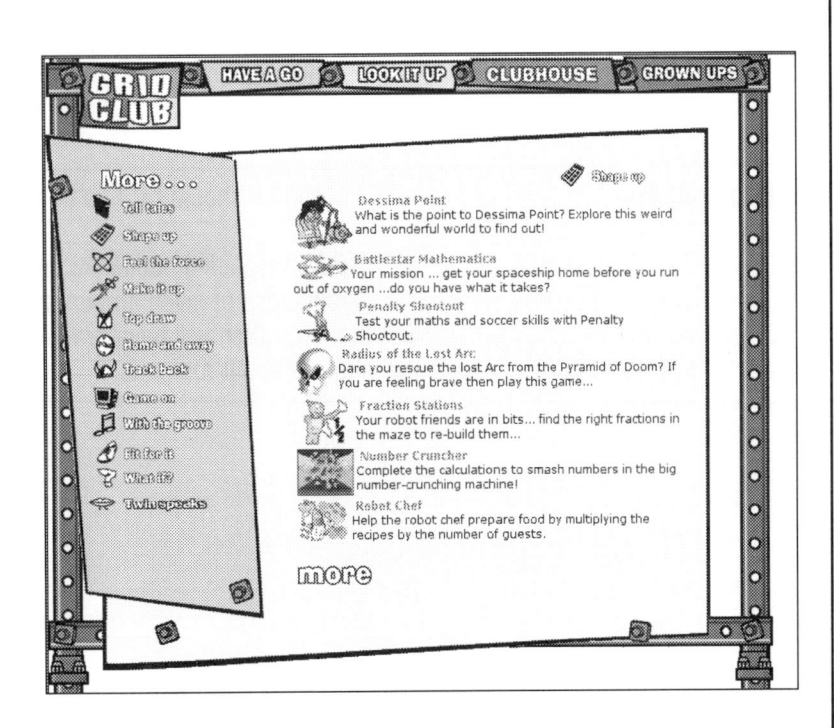

Unit 5 Money problems

Term Spring 2–3

Framework links

2–3	10	52–57	Understanding × and ÷	Consolidate all previous work.
		60–65	Mental calculation strategies (× and ÷)	Use brackets. Use factors. Use closely related facts. Partition, for example, 87× 6, 3.4 × 3.
		66–69	Pencil and paper procedures (× and ÷)	Extend written methods to short division of TU or HTU (mixed number answer) and of decimals.
		82–85	Money and "real-life" problems	Use all four operations to solve money or "real-life" word problems.
		70–75	Making decisions, checking results, including using a calculator	Choose appropriate operations/calculation methods. Explain working. Check by estimating. Use inverse operation, including with a calculator.

Setting the scene

It is the case that much of the calculating we do in our everyday lives concerns money and financing our activities. In this unit the children are offered a range of situations in which they have to calculate totals and amounts of money. They will be required to deploy not only problem solving skills but also to use the understanding they should now have of the four operations. As the children have developed a lot of mathematical experience and knowledge, the work here extends into the use of percentages of money.

Starting points

The children will be fully familiar with denominations of money and should be able to manipulate costs and totals. They have encountered percentage work before and should be able to calculate percentages of given totals. They will need to use all four operations.

Checking progress

- All children should be able to add, subtract and multiply amounts of money.
- Children requiring additional support will need help with calculating percentages of given amounts of money.
- Some children will have progressed further and will be able to make choices about methods.

Lesson 1

Learning objectives
Mental/oral starter:
- Derive sums and differences

Main teaching activities:
- Use all four operations to solve money problems
- Choose appropriate operations and calculations
- Check by estimating

Resources
A variety of shop and mail-order catalogues displaying goods with prices and code numbers, photocopies of Resource Sheet 27

Vocabulary
Digit, total, amount, estimate, money terms, operations terms

MENTAL/ORAL STARTER

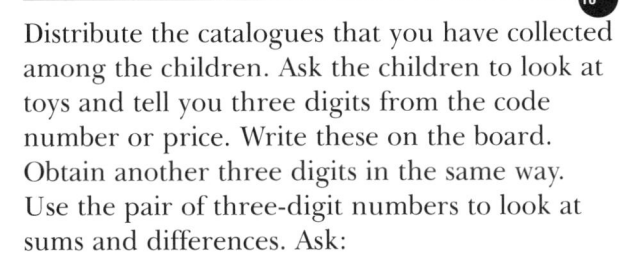

Distribute the catalogues that you have collected among the children. Ask the children to look at toys and tell you three digits from the code number or price. Write these on the board. Obtain another three digits in the same way. Use the pair of three-digit numbers to look at sums and differences. Ask:

How can we find the sum in our heads?

How can we find the difference?

Repeat the activity a number of times.

MAIN ACTIVITY

Whole class, individuals

Write £12.50 – £2.35 on the board. Show the children that it can be done like this: £10 + 50p – 35p = £10.15. Ask the children to tell you how this works.

Do the same problem this way: £12.50 – £2.50 = £10.00 + 15p = £10.15. Ask the children how this one works.

Write £135 × 8 on the board and ask for an estimate of the answer. Write the estimates down. Solve the multiplication by following these steps: £135 × 10 = £1 350 – 2 × £135 = £270 so our answer is £1 350 – £270 = £1 080. Ask how this works.

Solve the number sentence again: £150 times 8 equals £1 200, take away 8 times £15 equals £120, and £1 200 minus £120 equals £1 080. Again discuss how this works.

Tell the children:

In this lesson I want you to choose the best method to work out some money problems. Do an estimate first.

Give out Resource Sheet 27. Ask the children to work individually to solve the problems. If they find a particular question difficult, they should leave it for now.

■ Support
Discuss, with the children, specific methods for tackling the problems.

■ Challenge
Ask the children to find another way of working out the answers.

PLENARY

Work through some of the questions on the resource sheet. Invite individual children to explain how they got the answer. If there are alternative solutions share these too.

Key fact or strategy

Estimating an answer to a money problem is a useful starting point.

Lesson 2

◣ Learning objectives
Mental/oral starter:
- Add/subtract any pair of two-digit numbers, including crossing 100

Main teaching activities:
- Use all four operations to solve money problems
- Choose appropriate operations and calculations
- Check by using inverse operation, including with a calculator

📖 Resources
Photocopies of Resource Sheet 28, calculators

Vocabulary
Digit, total, amount, estimate, inverse, money terms, operations terms

MENTAL/ORAL STARTER

Give the children a short test on adding two-digit numbers. A suggested set of ten questions is shown here.

Two-digit number sentences

    37 + 53
    28 + 22
    19 + 39
    86 + 24
     4 + 97
    15 + 56
    91 + 11
    73 + 37
    58 + 58
    46 + 47

When these have been attempted, collect in the text sheets for evaluation. Now work through the solutions. Each of the ten shown is designed to demand different mental strategies for their solution so discuss how they were done as well as the answers.

MAIN ACTIVITY

Whole class, pairs

Write £3.25 on the board and ask the children what the result would be if we multiplied this amount by 6. Ask:

How did you do the calculation?

Write that for a concert 200 tickets were sold at £6.50 each. Ask:

How much money was received altogether?

Again discuss the strategies employed. Finally, write that people paid £4.50 for cinema tickets. The cinema took £900 altogether.

How many people saw the film?

How did you work out the answer?

Now go back over the examples you have given and ask how the answers could be checked – for example, we could divide the answer to the first one by 3.25 to see if the result is 6. Remind the children that we say that multiplication and division are inverse operations and so are addition and subtraction. Also remind them that estimation is a useful approach to use in thinking about the likely answer.

Give out Resource Sheet 28 to pairs of children. Ask them to work through it. They should give solutions and show how they have checked their answers. Ensure that calculators are available for making the final check.

■ Support
With the children, work through the first question and check the answer.

■ Challenge
Ask the children to invent another question linked to the River Festival.

PLENARY

Work through the resource sheet eliciting not only solutions but also how these were obtained and how they were checked.

Key fact or strategy
There is a range of ways for checking that a solution is correct.

Lesson 3

Learning objectives
Mental/oral starter:
- Derive sums and differences

Main teaching activities:
- Use all four operations to solve money problems
- Choose appropriate operations and calculations
- Check by using inverse operation, including with a calculator

Resources
Photocopies of Resource Sheet 29, photocopies of Resource Sheet 30 and Resource Sheet 31 (The latter provide the percentage cards and play money for the game on Resource Sheet 29. They need photocopying onto card or sticking on card and cutting up prior to the lesson.), dice, calculators, counters

Vocabulary
Percentage, digit, total, amount, estimate, inverse, money terms, operations terms

MENTAL/ORAL STARTER

Ask the children to give you a few pairs of two-digit numbers and use these to find sums and differences. Convert some of the two-digit numbers into three-digit numbers by multiplying by 10 and ask how we can do the sums and differences now. Use the same three-digit numbers but this time put digits other than zero in the units column. Discuss again how to derive sums and differences.

Does working out the two-digit answers help us?

Does making them end in zero help us with the three-digit numbers that do not end in zero?

MAIN ACTIVITY

Whole class, pairs

In this lesson the children play a track game that involves them in working out percentages of money. Start by doing a short revision of what percentages are and how we calculate them. A chart that the children could help you to complete is shown here.

Discounts

Price	2%	5%	10%
£50			
£100			
£125			
£200			

Give out the game, the cards and money for the children to play in pairs. Make calculators available as necessary to check the amounts that equate to the given percentages. The play money should be divided equally between the two players. The children should check how much they each have at the start. To play the game the children need a counter each. They should roll the dice and if they land on a percentage square they have to take a card and see what they have to do – give something to their opponent or to the bank. When one person gets to the end of the track both players should calculate what money they have left. The one with the most is the winner.

■ Support
Show the children how to calculate the percentages on the play cards.

■ Challenge
The children can work out the amount of money they would lose if they landed on all of the percentage squares.

PLENARY

Ask the children what was good about the game and what was less good. Ask the children about ways in which the game might be improved. Invite some children to tell you and the class how they calculated the amounts on the cards.

Key fact or strategy
Working out percentages of money is important in everyday life.

Supplementary activities

Mental/oral follow-up Develop a three-digit test along similar lines to the two-digit test. The questions should enable the children to use a variety of strategies to get the answers. Continued working on common number bonds will support the addition and subtraction of two- and three-digit numbers.

Homework Ask the children to complete Resource Sheet 32 at home. Use the catalogues that you have (include some school equipment catalogues if you wish) and ask the children to cost other related items for, say, an office or study and/or an alternative workstation.

Development Let the children play the percentage game again. Involve the children in producing new cards, a different track and situations where they receive as well as give percentages of sums of money.

ICT ideas *Homepages.Maths*.Year 6 (Nelson Thornes) includes a CD-ROM containing more than 80 ready-made worksheets that build into a comprehensive homework package. Each book also comes with a CD-ROM including editable versions of all the worksheets. Using this CD, the teacher can customise the worksheets (including many containing word problems) to meet the needs of individual children or use additional banks of prepared artwork for new contexts or consolidation work.

Unit 6 Measures problems

Term	Spring 7–8

Framework links

7–8	10	86–101	Measures including problems	Consolidate all previous work. Use formula for area of rectangle. Calculate the area of a shape formed from rectangles, including using a calculator with memory. Use, read and write standard metric units of mass and abbreviations. Know relationships. Convert larger to smaller units and vice versa. Know approximate metric equivalents for pounds (lb) and ounces (oz). Suggest suitable units and equipment to estimate or measure mass. Read measurements from scales.
		112–117	Handling data	Use all four operations to solve measurement word problems. Choose appropriate operations/calculation methods. Explain working. Represent, extract and interpret data in a line graph (for example, graph to convert miles to kilometres). Recognise that intermediate points have meaning.

Setting the scene	The predominant themes in this unit relate to metric mass and comparable imperial measures. The children are given a number of opportunities to convert from metric to imperial measures and vice versa. They make calculations involving masses and work with quantities in actual recipes. There is a passing reference to metric/imperial equivalents of volume.
Starting points	In Year 5/P6 the children will have worked with measures, including kilograms and grams, in "story" settings where they were expected to do addition, subtraction, multiplication and division. Earlier in this current year the children have tackled problems where length is used. In this unit they can build on what they know about mass.
Checking progress	■ All children should be comfortable with and confident in using grams and kilograms. They should be able to convert metric units to pounds and ounces and vice versa. ■ Children requiring additional support will need reminding of the mass equivalents in metric and imperial measures. ■ Some children will have progressed further and will be able to seek out recipes and make conversions from one kind of unit to another.

Lesson 1

Learning objectives
Mental/oral starter:
- Convert between kilometres and millimetres

Main teaching activities:
- Use addition, subtraction, multiplication and division to solve measures word problems involving grams and kilograms

Resources
Photocopies of Resource Sheet 33, calculators (These should be ready for the children to collect when they need them.), packs of dried foods of various masses (for Support), empty dried food packs with the mass in g stated on them (for Challenge)

Vocabulary
Kilometres, metres, centimetres, millimetres, kilograms, grams, convert

MENTAL/ORAL STARTER

Through quick-fire questioning, check that the children know the relationships between kilometres, metres, centimetres and millimetres. To confirm that they have a mental picture of these measures ask which unit they feel might be appropriate for measuring the following:

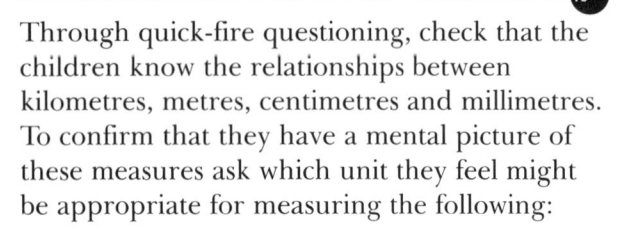

- the length of a curtain
- the length of a pin (commonly mm)
- a car journey
- a nail (commonly mm)
- a margin.

Write up on the board or call out a series of measurements, which they can convert from one to the other. Here is a list of challenges to begin the exercise.

km to mm

2 km	→	m
7 m	→	mm
106 cm	→	mm
2000 mm	→	m
0.1 km	→	cm
0.05 m	→	mm
4500 m	→	km

Compose some more challenges like this until the children are adept at making the conversion from one unit to another.

MAIN ACTIVITY

Whole class, individuals

Just as you have checked out the children's knowledge of the metric units of length now do the same with mass. The children should already know that we weigh in kilograms and grams, and that there are 1000 g in a kilogram and 2.2 lb. in a kilogram. They should remember that there are 16 ounces in a pound. Try out one or two addition and conversion examples.

What is 405 g plus 711 g? (1 kg 116 g)

What is 500 g in pounds/ounces? (1.1 lb or 18 oz approximately)

Give the children some example conversions that they can use in the lesson. Include:

- 1 kg is 2.2 lb
- 1 lb is just less than half a kg
- an ounce is usually converted to 25 g or 30 g as these are approximations.

Give out copies of Resource Sheet 33. The children work individually to do the comparisons, conversions and other challenges. They should use calculators only when they have attempted the arithmetic themselves.

■ Support
Give extra help to the children by showing them the dried foodstuffs of a range of masses. Talk them through the challenges and remind them of the information they already have regarding kg and lb.

■ **Challenge**

The children can check their work, where appropriate, with a calculator. Allow them to check out the packaging for the dried foods. They can work out:

1. What each full pack weighs in imperial measures.
2. What half the pack weighs in both measures.
3. What each of the smaller packs should weigh in a multi-pack.

PLENARY

Allow the children to sit with the completed resource sheets in front of them. Work through each challenge. Draw on the children's ideas for the solutions. Allow children who did not have access to the calculators in the lesson, the time to check the class answers where appropriate.

> **Key fact or strategy**
> There are 2.2 lb in a kg.

Lesson 2

> ■ **Learning objectives**
> *Mental/oral starter:*
> • Convert between kilograms and grams
> *Main teaching activities:*
> • Use addition, subtraction, multiplication and division to solve measures word problems involving grams and kilograms
>
> ■ **Resources**
> Photocopies of Resource Sheet 34
>
> ■ **Vocabulary**
> Kilogram, gram, addition, subtraction, multiplication, division, convert, rounding, estimation, millilitre

MENTAL/ORAL STARTER

Remind the children of all the work they did in the last lesson and confirm that they know the following facts.

- We weigh in kilograms and grams.
- There are 1 000 g in a kilogram.
- There are 2.2 lb in a kilogram.
- There are 16 ounces in a pound.

Give them some straightforward and some rather more tricky conversions from kilograms to grams and vice versa. Here are some example challenges.

kg to g

5 kg	→	g
1 kg	→	g
1000 g	→	kg
6000 g	→	kg
100 g	→	kg
0.5 kg	→	g
0.13 kg	→	g
55 g	→	kg

MAIN ACTIVITY

Whole class, individuals, pairs, small groups

Reiterate the facts used in the mental/oral session. Mention that we measure volume in millilitres and litres and that there are 5 millilitres in a teaspoon (the children will need this information to do the work on the resource sheet).

Remind the children of the concept of rounding, where we determine a number or quantity as an approximation that is easier to work with. We sometimes use rounding when making conversions from imperial to metric measures and vice versa.

Discuss the concept of estimation. Estimation enables us to make important and quick decisions in everyday life. We can determine how many helpings a recipe will make, how much of an item to shop for, how much to put in if we vary a recipe.

Give every child a copy of Resource Sheet 34. Ask the children to copy out the recipe ingredients into their exercise books. As they do so, they should convert the amounts to metric units.

Bring the class together and work through the recipes. Make all the conversions, with the children's help, and discuss the methods used. Below are the conversion details suggested in the recipes. They are approximations and the preferred conversions in class may not exactly correspond with these. This provides another opportunity to talk about rounding.

Recipe conversions

Apple flapjack

2 oz (50 g) margarine
2 level tbsp golden syrup
2 oz (50 g) demerara sugar
6 oz (175 g) rolled oats

Filling
1 oz (25 g) margarine
1 lb (450 g) cooking apples
2 oz (50 g) granulated sugar

Apricot sponge

6 oz (175 g) margarine
6 oz (175 g) Barbados sugar
3 large eggs
6 oz (175 g) wholemeal self-raising flour
1 heaped tbsp apricot ham in 4 tsp water

Filling
3 oz (75 g) margarine
2 oz (50 g) sugar
2 tbsp apricot jam

Tiger biscuits

4 oz (100 g) plain flour
4 oz (100 g) margarine
1 oz (25 g) caster sugar

Filling
1½ oz (40 g) margarine
1½ oz (40 g) icing sugar, sieved
½ tsp coffee essence
2oz (50 g) almonds

■ **Support**
The children may benefit from working out the conversions in pairs.

■ **Challenge**
The children can work out the quantities of ingredients if the recipe is doubled or halved.

PLENARY

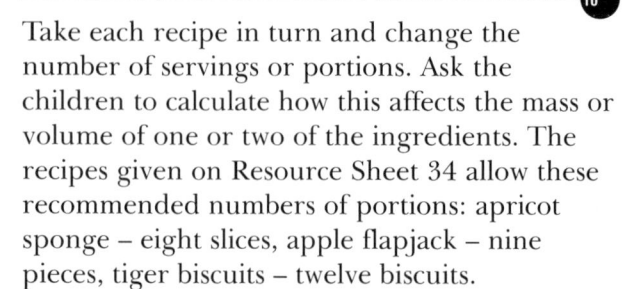

Take each recipe in turn and change the number of servings or portions. Ask the children to calculate how this affects the mass or volume of one or two of the ingredients. The recipes given on Resource Sheet 34 allow these recommended numbers of portions: apricot sponge – eight slices, apple flapjack – nine pieces, tiger biscuits – twelve biscuits.

Key fact or strategy
The facts listed in the mental/oral starter are important, along with rounding and estimation.

Supplementary activities

Mental/oral follow-up Remind the children of the conversions they have done between kilometres and millimetres and between kilograms and grams. Link these conversions to other kinds of conversions: between metric and imperial units; between litres, millilitres and pints; between seconds, minutes and hours. Give the children oral challenges relating to these conversions. Short tests involving conversions can be set up.

Homework Give the children a copy of Resource Sheet 35 to complete at home. This can be returned to school for classroom discussion.

Development Give the children the opportunity to search out recipes, assemble the ingredients and cook them. They can try using imperial and metric measures but must remember not to mix them in the same recipe. They can experiment in halving and doubling recipes, predict the outcomes and test them in "real life".

ICT ideas BBC *Maths Workshop Shape and Space* CD-ROM includes some differentiated activities covering length, mass and capacity, as well as some area and perimeter and time problems.

Children should be encouraged to use a calculator to solve problems involving measures – particularly conversions work similar to that on Resource Sheet 34. This work might be incorporated into their calculations work in the Spring term.

Unit 7 Handling data

Term				Spring 7–8	

Framework links

7–8	10	86–101	Measures including problems	Consolidate all previous work. Use formula for area of rectangle. Calculate the area of a shape formed from rectangles, including using a calculator with memory. Use, read and write standard metric units of mass and abbreviations. Know relationships. Convert larger to smaller units and vice versa. Know approximate metric equivalents for pounds (lb) and ounces (oz). Suggest suitable units and equipment to estimate or measure mass. Read measurements from scales. Use all four operations to solve measurement word problems. Choose appropriate operations/calculation methods. Explain worklng.
		112–117	Handling data	Represent, extract and interpret data in a line graph (for example, graph to convert miles to kilometres). Recognise that intermediate points have meaning.

Setting the scene	The children have already had a variety of experiences concerning the pictorial representation of data. In early years they have worked with block graphs then moved onto bar charts. These in turn have been developed as bar line graphs where the points at the top of each line have become particularly significant. The children have had some experience of seeing that different representations work best in different circumstances. They should know something about the differences that discrete and continuous data make. In this unit we focus exclusively on line graphs, which means that all of the data encountered is continuous. The children start by drawing and using line graphs of multiplication, then move onto looking at some conversion graphs. Finally a range of line graphs is offered, some of which are inappropriate and the children have to discuss the merits and demerits of the proffered representations.
Starting points	The children need to use their knowledge of times tables. They also need to use their experience of using x and y axes, appropriately labelled and scaled. Reading data from charts and graphs will be important in this unit.
Checking progress	■ All children should be familiar with the use of axes for graphs and how to use these to make charts and graphs, or read from them. ■ Children requiring additional support will need help with scaling. ■ Some children will have progressed further and will readily see the context for scaling.

Lesson 1

Learning objectives

Mental/oral starter:
- Multiply or divide whole numbers by 10, 100 and 1000

Main teaching activities:
- Represent, extract and interpret data in a line graph
- Recognise that intermediate points have meaning

Resources
Photocopies of General Resource Sheet B (enough for two copies for each child), an OHT of General Resource Sheet B, rulers, sharp pencils

Vocabulary
Line graph, multiplication, axis, axes, scale, label

MENTAL/ORAL STARTER

Use the examples shown here to multiply by 10, 100 and 1000.

10, 100 and 1000 times

- My pet snail raced 3 cm in a minute yesterday. How far in 10 minutes? ... 100 minutes? ... 1000 minutes? How long is 100/1000 minutes?
- My pet hamster can turn his wheel 2½ times in 1 second. How many in 10 seconds? ... 100 seconds? ... 1000 seconds? How long is 100/1000 seconds?
- My pet elephant can eat 96 buns in a day. How many in 10 days? ... 100 days? ... 1000 days? How long is 100/1000 days?

MAIN ACTIVITY

Whole class, pairs

Display the OHT of General Resource Sheet B. Tell the children that you want to make a graph of the 5 times table. Ask:
What do I need to do?

With the help of the children produce a graph like the one shown here.

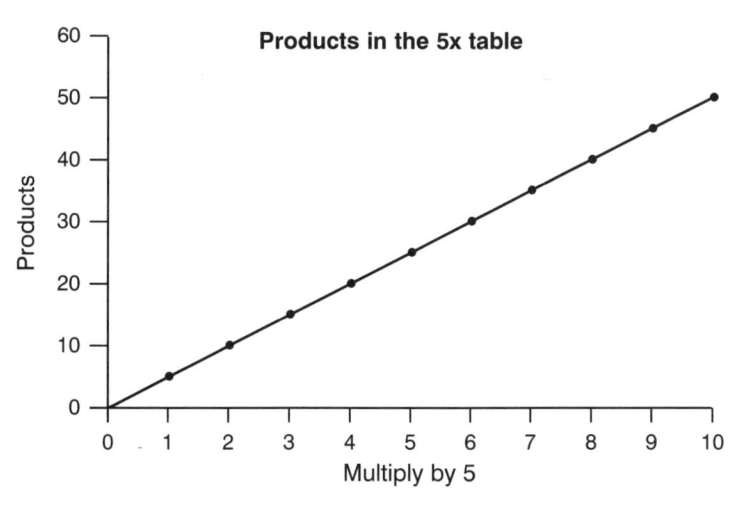

Discuss the axes and the scale. Ask:
Could we use this line graph to help us work out a greater multiplication than 5 × 10?

Can we use it to help us work out, say, 5 × 2.5?

Tell the children that you want them to have a go at drawing a times table line graph. Give out General Resource Sheet B, rulers and sharp pencils. Remind the children that they need to think about what numbers to put on each scale to make a times 7 line graph. When the children have attempted this, use an OHT of General Resource Sheet B to plot your own version. Discuss the axes and scaling.

Give out another copy of General Resource Sheet B and ask the children to try drawing the times 9 graph.

- **Support**
Help the children with the scaling of the axes.

- **Challenge**
Ask the children to draw the 8 times table on the same graph as the 9 times table.

PLENARY

Use an OHT of General Resource Sheet B and ask the children to help you to draw the times 9 line graph. Ask:

What is 8 × 9?

Check this on your graph.

What is 5½ times 9?

Can you give me an estimate for 3.25 times 9?

What would we need to do if we wanted to use the graph to work out 12.5 times 9? Why can we draw a line between the points on this sort of graph?

> **Key fact or strategy**
> Line graphs of multiplication tables are a good basis for later work on graphs.

Lesson 2

> **Learning objectives**
> *Mental/oral starter:*
> • Round decimals to the nearest whole number or nearest tenth
> *Main teaching activities:*
> • Represent, extract and interpret data in a line graph
> • Recognise that intermediate points have meaning
>
> **Resources**
> Photocopies of Resource Sheet 36, an OHT of Resource Sheet 36, photocopies of Resource Sheet 37, road atlases, ordinary atlases (You may wish to make an enlargement or an OHT of the mileage chart used in the main activity.) It may also be helpful to have mileage charts for other cities in the UK for challenge and extension work.
>
> **Vocabulary**
> Miles, kilometres, mileage, distance, convert, conversion, line graph

MENTAL/ORAL STARTER

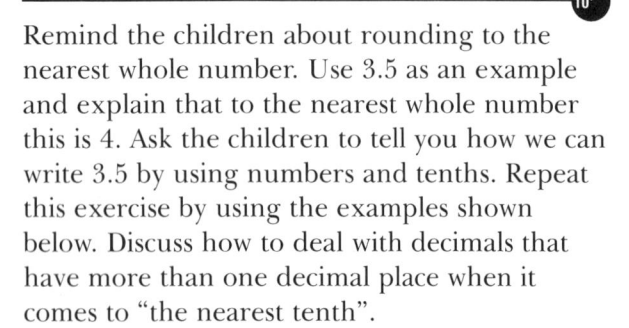

Remind the children about rounding to the nearest whole number. Use 3.5 as an example and explain that to the nearest whole number this is 4. Ask the children to tell you how we can write 3.5 by using numbers and tenths. Repeat this exercise by using the examples shown below. Discuss how to deal with decimals that have more than one decimal place when it comes to "the nearest tenth".

Round decimals – whole numbers and tenths

6.5	7	$6^{5}/_{10}$ or $6^{1}/_{2}$
3.25	3	$3^{3}/_{10}$
19.52	19	$19^{5}/_{10}$ or $19^{1}/_{2}$
17.17	17	$17^{2}/_{10}$ or $17^{1}/_{5}$

MAIN ACTIVITY

Whole class, pairs

Use part of a mileage grid to show the children how to read off the distance between places. An example is shown here.

Mileage chart

100	Gloucester			
31	133	Guildford		
216	301	156	Hereford	
197	241	200	220	Holyhead
				Hull

(Hereford is 156 miles from Holyhead.)

Now show the children the OHT of Resource Sheet 36. Ask:

By using what you have learned from the multiplication line graphs you made, can you tell me how to use this conversion graph?

Give out Resource Sheet 37 and tell the children to work in pairs to choose some places on here and find them in their atlases. They should write down the places that they choose then work out the distances between them in both miles and kilometres. When they have done this, invite different pairs to tell the class some locations and the distance between them. Check out the answers by using the mileage chart and the conversion graph.

■ **Support**

Read off the mileage between some places and then help the children to convert these by using Resource Sheet 36.

■ **Challenge**

The children can use a road atlas to work out some local journeys in miles and then convert to kilometres by using the conversion graph.

PLENARY

Choose three places and say to the class where you are starting, where you are going and where you are going from there. Ask pairs to look up distances and work out your total mileage. Then ask them to convert this to kilometres. Do this a few times. Finish by asking:

Why is it possible for us to draw this conversion graph as a line graph?

Key fact or strategy
Graphs and charts are very practical tools for working out conversions such as miles to kilometres and vice versa.

Lesson 3

Learning objectives
Mental/oral starter:
- Know some fractions as percentages/decimals
- Find simple percentages

Main teaching activities:
- Represent, extract and interpret data in a line graph
- Recognise that intermediate points have meaning

Resources
Dienes apparatus, colour factor resources or Cuisenaire rods (If these are not available, cut out some strips, keep one whole and cut the others into fractions such as halves, quarters, thirds and so on.), photocopies of Resource Sheets 38 and 39, and General Resource Sheet D, an OHT of the line graph produced from the data on Resource Sheet 39

Vocabulary
Fraction, percentage, decimal, decibel, line graph, distance, time

MENTAL/ORAL STARTER

Place a long Cuisenaire rod on the OHP and use smaller rods to make fractions of the whole. Ask the children to tell you what fraction the smaller pieces are and what percentage of the whole that is. Do the same with Dienes apparatus.

MAIN ACTIVITY

Whole class, pairs

Give out Resource Sheet 38. Explain that by using a temperature sensor attached to a computer, the temperature readings were obtained for a 24-hour period. Organise the children to work in pairs to discuss the possible answers to the questions. When they have done this, go through the questions with the whole class.

Write up the information relating to time and distance which appears on Resource Sheet 39 on the board if necessary.

Give each child a copy of Resource Sheet 39, although the children continue to work in pairs. Also give them a sheet of graph paper (as on General Resource Sheet D). Tell the class:

You have to draw a line graph to display the data. When you have done this try to answer the questions.

■ Support
Help the children with the scaling of the journey graph on Resource Sheet 39.

■ Challenge
Ask the children to devise some more questions based on the graphs from Resource Sheets 38 and 39.

PLENARY

Display the OHT you have made to compare the line graph with the graphs that the children have produced. Discuss the answers to the questions.

> **Key fact or strategy**
> Line graphs are often a good way of representing information that involves time.

Supplementary activities

Mental/oral follow-up

Use the examples from the mental/oral starter in Lesson 1 to stimulate the children to make up some of their own numbers to round. They can try these out on the class or you can put their suggestions up on display for opportunistic practice.

The children can cut strips of paper to make fractions of a whole and label these as fractions, decimals and percentages.

Homework

Give out Resource Sheet 40. Explain to the children that they should use the conversion graph to help them to answer the questions.

Development

Encourage the children to collect graphs from magazines and newspapers. These can be displayed and discussed. It is important to note that some graphs in the press are of discrete data and should not really be presented as line graphs.

Ask the children to make "ready reckoner" line graphs for multiplication tables on one sheet of graph paper and/or graphs of 12, 15 times tables.

ICT ideas

Let the children do some data collection by using sensors. These could be sound, heat or light sensors. The data should be presented in a line graph (many sensor kits produce such graphs on the computer).

The temperature conversion chart on Resource Sheet 40 could be prepared using a spreadsheet program. You might support the children in this work by creating the structure of the spreadsheet, leaving the children to input the data values and create the graph. Make sure the children understand that the intermediate points of the line graph have meaning. The children could also be asked to find some up-to-date weather information using Internet sites such as the Met Office (www.metoffice.com). The children could then use this data to compare daily temperatures from two different cities.

You might give the children a prepared set of data within a database or spreadsheet and ask them to try different methods of representation for both continuous and discrete data. Children should now be adept at contrasting different methods of presentation and deciding upon the most appropriate for each set of data.

Further ICT ideas involving the use of line graphs with intermediate values can be found in Unit 9.

Unit 8   "Real-life" problems

Term   Spring 9–10

Framework links

9–10	10	40–47	Mental calculation strategies (+ and –)	Consolidate all previous work.
		48–51	Pencil and paper procedures (+ and –)	Extend written methods to column + and – of numbers involving decimals.
		82–85	Money and "real-life" problems	Use all four operations to solve word problems involving money or "real-life" measurement.
		70–75	Making decisions and checking results, including using a calculator	Choose appropriate operations/calculation methods. Explain working. Check by adding in reverse order, including with a calculator.

Setting the scene

The lessons in this unit have been arranged in a way that gives the children experience in working with numbers and measures in "real life". The first lesson uses real data for practice in the addition and subtraction of decimals. The following lesson requires the use of numbers and measures. The final two lessons are to be treated as a pair and rely on the children having access to data sources in school. The possibilities for data collection will depend on the setting and composition of the school.

Starting points

In all these lessons the children should be using their established knowledge to determine what kinds of operation are required to solve problems, and to carry them through, sometimes with the aid of a calculator. The children should be familiar with problems involving numbers and measures. They should, therefore, know how to tackle the problems in these lessons.

Checking progress

- All children should realise that we solve problems in everyday life by using just the same strategies as they are using in class. They should be able to choose and use appropriate operations in the solution of problems.
- Children requiring additional support will need to be reminded why learning to solve problems is useful. They will need help in seeing the steps through to problem solution.
- Some children will have progressed further and will be able to readily detect everyday data that is useful for "real-life" problem creation and create problems using this data.

Lesson 1

Learning objectives
Mental/oral starter:
- Find decimals with a sum of 0.1 or 1

Main teaching activities:
- Use addition and/or subtraction to solve "real-life" problems
- Choose appropriate operations

Resources
A set of decimal flashcards with numbers from 0.01 to 0.99 on them (They should be made up before the lesson. They can be numbered 0.01, 0.02, 0.03, 0.04 … 0.10, 0.11, 0.12 … 0.25, 0.26, and so on. The flashcards can be set aside as a resource for this and other mental/oral sessions.), photocopies of Resource Sheet 41

Vocabulary
Decimal, pair, sum, decimal point, two decimal places

MENTAL/ORAL STARTER

Sort the decimal flashcards by taking only those numbered from 0.01 to 0.09. Shuffle these flashcards. Write 0.1 in large numerals on the board. Tell the children that this is the total they are to work with. Hold up a decimal card at random. If, for example, it is 0.04, ask:

What do we need to add to this to make 0.1? (0.06)

Write 0.04 and 0.06 on the board as a pair.

Take another decimal card at random and ask the same question.

Halfway through the mental/oral time, pick up all the decimal flashcards that were set aside at the beginning of the session and shuffle them. Write 1 on the board in place of 0.1. Take a card at random and ask what needs to be added to it to make 1. Do this a number of times.

MAIN ACTIVITY

Whole class, individuals, small groups

In this lesson the data on the resource sheet is real information. There are percentages here but the arithmetic involves the children in recognising, adding and subtracting decimals.

Extend the work done in the mental/oral starter by writing up any decimal (to two decimal places) on the board, and then setting a total for which the children need to find the pair number. Here is an example.

23.67   total to make 50.50

Answer: $50.50 - 23.67 = 26.83$

Such examples are more complex than the work on Resource Sheet 41. They can be worked through with the children's help. Give ample opportunities to discuss the methods that work.

Give out Resource Sheet 41. Allow the children some time to tackle it individually. Later, they can then get together in groups to work up a set of model answers.

■ Support
Lead the children through the worksheet challenges one at a time.

■ Challenge
The children can take the worksheet challenges further by making some resources (such as posters and display statistics) to address the final challenge on the resource sheet.

PLENARY

Use this session as an opportunity to go through the resource sheet work and set out strategies for adding and subtracting decimals.

> **Key fact or strategy**
> Take care to note the position of the decimal point when computing with decimals.

Lesson 2

Learning objectives
Mental/oral starter:
- Find halves of decimals ending in an even digit

Main teaching activities:
- Use addition, subtraction, multiplication and division to solve "real-life" measurement problems

Resources
Brochures and specification information about bicycles and/or cars (These should be collected beforehand for use in the introduction to the lesson.), calculators, photocopies of Resource Sheet 42

Vocabulary
Decimal, decimal point, even, digit, addition, subtraction, multiplication, division

MENTAL/ORAL STARTER

This is the first of three consecutive mental/oral starters working on decimals ending in an even digit. Use this first session to discuss why it is that decimals like this can be halved easily. Your contribution to the discussion may begin as follows:

What is half 2.6? ... 4.8? ... 5.4?

Why is it that these numbers were easy to halve neatly?

What is an even number?

What are all the digits that we could have at the end of the number so that it is easily halved?

MAIN ACTIVITY

Whole class, individuals, pairs

The context used here for creating "real-life" number and measurement problems is transport: bicycles, buses and cars. Brochures relating to bicycles or cars can yield real numbers and measurements that can be used to set up examples to work through on the board.

After several examples have been discussed, give each child a copy of Resource Sheet 42 to work through individually. Once they have completed it, they can work with a partner and a calculator to check their answers.

■ Support
The children should tackle Resource Sheet 42 as a group. They can do each calculation in turn. Before starting the work they should ask:

1. What am I finding out?
2. What kinds of operation do I need?
3. What special strategies can I use (estimation, rounding, reverse operations to check the answer, and so on)?

■ Challenge
Give the children the bicycle brochures to look at in pairs. They can use the data to try to create more "real-life" measurement problems.

PLENARY

Review those parts of the work on the resource sheet that the children found difficult to do.

Key fact or strategy

Decide on the operations before beginning an attempt to solve a problem.

Lesson 3

Learning objectives
Mental/oral starter:
- Find halves of decimals ending in an even digit

Main teaching activities:
- Collect data to use in solving "real-life" problems

Resources
Photocopy Resource Sheet 43, an OHT of Resource Sheet 43 (for use in the mental/oral starter), access to all parts of the school (In this lesson extra adult help would be invaluable to support the children with access to other parts of the school.)

Vocabulary
Decimal, decimal point, even, digit, addition, subtraction, multiplication, division

MENTAL/ORAL STARTER

Display the OHT of Resource Sheet 43 to show the children the digits in the left-hand column. Each of these can be joined to any of the decimal numbers occurring after the decimal point, for example, 33 can become 33.6, 33.12, 33.78, and so on.

After making each number, ask the children to halve it. Remind them that each ends in an even number. Some of these numbers are tricky and the children would benefit from the opportunity to work them out as a class so that the steps in division can be emphasised.

MAIN ACTIVITY

Whole class, small groups

Take the opportunity in this lesson to set up and carry through a school-based investigation that yields data from which "real-life" problems can be devised. If appropriate, send off small groups of children, accompanied by an adult, to conduct an investigation. Here is a list of suggestions that might prove useful starting points for an investigation.

- How much glass is there in school?
- How long does it take to clean the windows?
- What is the total floor area in all the classrooms?

- What are the orders made by kitchen staff for milk? potatoes? ... custard powder?
- How often are food orders placed?
- How do the kitchen staff estimate the quantities they need?

Interview the school ICT co-ordinator to obtain information like this:
- How many printer cartridges are ordered at a time?
- How many sheets of paper are used over a fixed period?
- In what quantities are paper bought?

While the investigations progress, the children's own ideas for key questions can be incorporated into the work.

The purpose here is data gathering. The children will then be able to use this data in the lesson that follows.

■ Support
When investigation tasks are assigned, the children would benefit from a clearly defined task and copious adult support.

■ Challenge
There will be plenty of opportunities for the children to collate important data.

PLENARY

Bring all the children together and start to collate the data they have collected. Detail the information and numbers that can be used to create or solve challenges in the next lesson.

Key fact or strategy
Mathematical data is all around us and it is useful to be able to interpret it.

Lesson 4

Learning objectives

Mental/oral starter:
- Find halves of decimals ending in an even digit

Main teaching activities:
- Create and solve "real-life" problems
- Use addition, subtraction, multiplication and/or division to solve "real-life" problems
- Choose appropriate operations
- Check the answers by adding in reverse order, including with a calculator

Resources
Access to all parts of the school (Extra adult help would be invaluable.), calculators

Vocabulary
Decimal, decimal point, even, digit, addition, subtraction, multiplication, division

MENTAL/ORAL STARTER

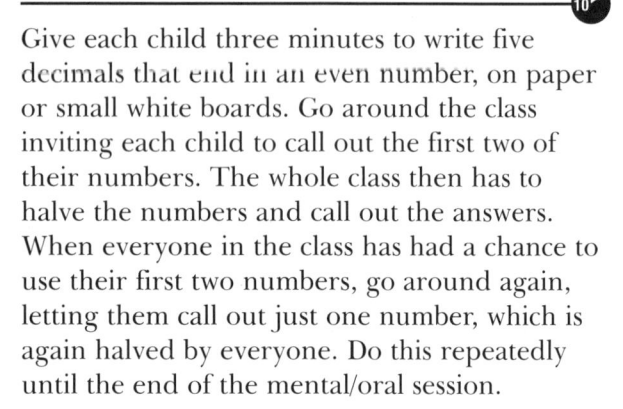

Give each child three minutes to write five decimals that end in an even number, on paper or small white boards. Go around the class inviting each child to call out the first two of their numbers. The whole class then has to halve the numbers and call out the answers. When everyone in the class has had a chance to use their first two numbers, go around again, letting them call out just one number, which is again halved by everyone. Do this repeatedly until the end of the mental/oral session.

MAIN ACTIVITY

Whole class, small groups

Collect and lay out the data from the previous lesson. If it has not been collated and no "real-life" problems have been devised, allow the children, in their groups, to do this. If data is still required groups can be directed to collect this, with extra adult support.

When there are "real-life" problems devised from the data the children have collected, ready to be solved, either organise the children to work in groups or call the whole class together to work out the problems. Give the children the chance to check calculations with reverse operations and use calculators where necessary.

■ Support
Allow the children to work under close supervision so that they can be supported through data collection, problem derivation and solution.

■ Challenge
The children can continue to suggest, derive and solve meaningful problems throughout the lesson.

PLENARY

Discuss with the children the kinds of problems they solve in their everyday lives. Here are some examples.

- Have I the time to finish my homework before watching TV?
- How far away is my friend's new house?

Key fact or strategy
Knowledge of problem-solving strategies is useful in everyday life.

Supplementary activities

Mental/oral follow-up Rehearse the special features of odd and even numbers and practise halving whole numbers, numbers with one decimal place, and numbers with two decimal places.

Homework Ask the children to do some investigation into the tinned goods they have in their home. They can create a project file, collect wrappers, and devise "real-life" problems related to these. They may choose tinned fruit, tinned vegetables or pet food and look at:
- the number of tins and total mass purchased each week/month/year
- the comparative mass of tins of different products
- the comparative content of starch/protein in different cans
- the costs of foods.

Development Have fun determining and using specific class data. Here are some suggestions.

If all our journeys to school/heights were laid end to end how long would that be?

What is the estimated weight of all our pet dogs and cats? How can we find out?

What percentage of our mums are less than 1.6 m tall? How can we find out?

ICT ideas The activities in the Supplementary activities section offer opportunities to collect and represent (estimated) data using a computer database. Use the facilities of the database to compare and contrast the presentation of data.

Invite the children to evaluate the following program. For which age group do they think it would be suitable? Although intended originally as part of the Microelectronics Education Programme (MEP) Infant Pack, the *Play Train* program (part of the *Using ICT to support mathematics* pack) is a number puzzle program for all ages. The children have to fill train carriages with passengers using a restricted set of numbers.

Unit 9   Money problems

Term   Summer 2–3

Framework links

2–3	10	52–57	Understanding × and ÷	Consolidate all previous work. Express a quotient as a fraction, or as a decimal rounded to 1 decimal place. Dividing £ and pence by a two-digit number to give £ and pence. Round up or down after division depending on the context.
		60–65	Mental calculation strategies (× and ÷)	Use known facts and place value to multiply and divide mentally. Use relationship between multiplication and division.
		66–69	Pencil and paper procedures (× and ÷)	Multiply HTU by TU. Division HTU by TU (long division, whole number answer).
		82–85	Money and "real-life" problems	Use all four operations to solve word problems involving money or "real life" including finding percentages and VAT.
		70–75	Making decisions and checking results, including using a calculator	Choose appropriate operations/calculation methods. Explain working. Check using products of odd/even numbers or doing the inverse calculation, including using a calculator.

Setting the scene

In this unit we concentrate on money problems and in so doing we make use of a variety of experiences that the children have had earlier in the year. These experiences include not only calculations and work in all four operations but also work on percentages and conversions from one unit to another. Specifically the lessons in the unit deal with finding percentages of amounts, conversions between currencies and the application of percentages to such things as saving and borrowing, and purchasing. All of these matters are, of course, very much a part of our everyday lives.

Starting points

The children have had experience in calculating fractions, decimals and percentages. They have also had a good range of work concerning money and money problems. Most children will have heard of, and indeed experienced, the need to buy foreign currency when travelling abroad. There will be opportunities to discuss the advent of the euro in a number of European countries.

Checking progress

- All children should be able to discuss what we mean by percentage and indicate how this might be calculated/or how it relates to fractions of an amount or quantity.
- Children requiring additional support will need help in calculating percentages of given amounts.
- Some children will have progressed further and will be able to handle ideas such as VAT on a purchase.

Lesson 1

Learning objectives
Mental/oral starter:
- Add and subtract any pair of two-digit numbers including crossing 100

Main teaching activities:
- Use all four number operations to solve word problems involving money including finding percentages

Resources
Telephone directory or directories, five items that can be priced (Examples could be brought into school, say, a book at £10, a sweater at £25, and so on, or you could identify and price five items in the classroom.), photocopies of Resource Sheet 44

Vocabulary
Digit, percentage, discount, commission

MENTAL/ORAL STARTER

One of the difficulties in generating two-digit numbers is to keep the process fresh. Here you can make use of a telephone directory or directories. Invite individual children to read out a phone number at random then split this into pairs of digits. Use these randomly selected two-digit numbers to mentally sum and subtract.

MAIN ACTIVITY

Whole class, pairs

Display the five items that you have brought in or identify five objects in the classroom. Tell the children the price of an item and ask:

If there was a 10% discount, how much would it cost?

What if you managed to get a 20% discount?

Choose another item and give its price. Tell the children:

This has gone up in price by 5%. How much would it cost now?

Continue this sort of process with other items using 15%, 1%, 50%, and so on. When you feel that the children are ready, give copies of Resource Sheet 44 to pairs of children. Ask everyone to read the introduction.

What do you think commission means?

When the children are clear about this, ask them to work through the questions.

■ Support
Do some more work with the children on ways of working out percentages of amounts.

■ Challenge
Tell the children that in one year Colin had annual sales of £16 000. What is his total commission? What is that as a percentage of £16 000?

PLENARY

Work through the resource sheet. If there are answers that are not in accord then work through the calculation in detail. Invite the children to suggest strategies and processes. Collect in the work for checking.

Key fact or strategy
Finding 1% (one hundredth) and then multiplying this by the number of percentage points required can be a useful way of doing percentages of amounts.

Lesson 2

Learning objectives
Mental/oral starter:
- Derive sums and differences

Main teaching activities:
- Use all four number operations to solve word problems involving money
- Use a calculator or written method to convert foreign currency

Resources
A newspaper that has a section where car registration numbers are for sale and/or a survey of the car registrations of staff cars, photocopies of Resource Sheet 45, the pages from today's newspaper that give the current exchange rates for a range of different currencies (You could contact a local bank or travel agent to obtain this day's rates for the currencies used on Resource Sheet 45.)

Vocabulary
Digits, place value, exchange rates

MENTAL/ORAL STARTER

Invite individual children to generate some two-digit numbers from the car registration numbers. Take a pair of these and do the sums and differences, for example, 43 and 35 would give a sum of 78 and a difference of 8. Use the same pair of numbers, multiply them by ten and ask the children to sum 430 and 350. Ask:

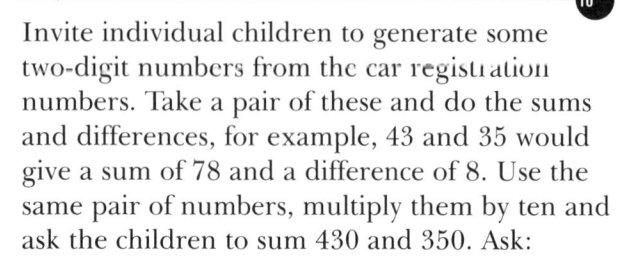

What is the difference between 430 and 350?

Use the same pair of starting numbers. Ask the children:

What is the sum of 4.3 and 3.5?
What is the difference?

Can the children explain how these three computations connect? That is, the digits move place and acquire a different place value. Repeat the exercise with other pairs of two-digit numbers.

MAIN ACTIVITY
Whole class, individuals

Ask the children:

If you go to another country for a visit or holiday what do you need to do about having some money to use there?
How do you know how much money you will get for, say, £20?

Write exchange rates on the board at some point in the discussion and explain what this means.

Give out copies of Resource Sheet 45. Tell the children to look at the exchange rates.

How many Australian dollars are equivalent to £1, ... £2, ... £5?

How many US dollars are equivalent to £5?

Tell the children: *I want you to price the goods shown here in at least two other currencies, for example, the sweater in euros and Japanese yen.*

When the children have made sufficient progress, invite different pairs to share their results with the class. The class should check each time.

■ Support
The children work in a group. They choose one item on the resource sheet in turn and work through how its price can be converted into some of the other currencies.

■ Challenge
Give the newspaper with the range of exchange rates to the children and ask them to explore other currencies that have not been used in the lesson.

PLENARY

Use the day's newspaper or the information you have obtained about current exchange rates to compare with the ones given on Resource Sheet 45. Discuss why there might be differences and that currencies can change on a day-to-day basis.

> **Key fact or strategy**
> Exchange rates are used to convert one currency to another. In countries using the Euro, exchange rates are necessary only for currencies outside the Euro-zone.

Lesson 3

Learning objectives

Mental/oral starter:
- Find decimals with a sum of 0.1, 1 or 10

Main teaching activities:
- Use all four number operations to solve word problems involving money
- Calculate simple percentages using a calculator

Resources

A selection of local newspapers, a collection of advertisements (Some examples are given below.)

Something to sell?
Advertise in the 'Local Leader'
Your price	Advert price
..up to £200	£2 inc.VAT
£201–£300	£3 inc.VAT
£301+	£5 inc.VAT

Homesafe Estate Agents
Let us manage your properties
..... rents collected.
.... maintenance.
.. agreements drawn up.

12% + VAT

Brian the Builder
Tell us.. we'll build it!
Estimates Free
No job too small
Vat Registered

The Olive Tree
Mediterranean Cuisine
Vast menu • Parties catered for • service charge 12½%

Dickens and Brown Solicitors
Care and Service
Reasonable rates

Photocopies of Resource Sheet 46, calculators

Vocabulary

Percentage, service charge, estimate, rate, VAT, total, cost

MENTAL/ORAL STARTER

Ask the children to tell you two decimals that sum to 10, then two more and a further two. Ask if they can tell you three decimals that sum to 10. Ask:

Will the answers to these help you to tell me two/three decimals that sum to 1?

Use the answers given so far and then ask for other pairs and triples of decimals that sum to 1.

Will the answers to all of these help you to tell me two/three decimals that sum to 0.1?

Again use existing answers and then see whether the children can expand the set.

MAIN ACTIVITY

Whole class, pairs

Show some of the pages that deal with house sales in the newspapers that you have collected. Ask:

How might readers use these pages?

Concentrate on prices, descriptions and localities. Explain that estate agents make their money by charging house sellers a percentage of the price they get when the agent sells the house. Give an example of a £50 000 or £100 000 house where the agent charges 1%. Repeat this for an agent charging $1\frac{1}{2}$%. Use further prices and include some of the real ones in the paper where the numbers are appropriate.

Explain to the children that it is not just estate agents who charge percentages – we all pay VAT on many of the things that we buy. Explain what VAT is. Discuss other charges based on the advertisements that you have prepared. Tell the children: *Now I want you to see whether you can work out some of the costs and charges for different services.*

Give out copies of Resource Sheet 46 and calculators. Organise the children to work in pairs to tackle the questions on the resource sheet.

■ Support

Work through the first example with the children and/or provide some amounts and calculate VAT at $17\frac{1}{2}$% on these.

■ Challenge

Ask the children to find examples of percentages, including VAT, in the local newspapers.

PLENARY

Go through the resource sheet (if you have one you can put an OHP calculator on display). Invite different pairs to help you with the solutions. Where the children have further queries about the services, answer those that are straightforward but reserve those that are more complex for a follow-up session.

> **Key fact or strategy**
> Percentages are commonly used to give the same proportion but on different amounts.

Supplementary activities

Mental/oral follow-up Start to do more additions where there are three numbers to handle rather than two. Discuss strategies for adding up columns of numbers. Find decimals that make 0.5 and 5, and 0.2 and 2.

Homework Give out copies of Resources Sheet 47.

Development Ask the children to find out all that they can about three different currencies. They should include exchange rates with the pound sterling and exchange rates between the currencies. Some example currencies are shown here.

Some major national currencies	
Bulgaria	lev
Chile	Chilean peso
Finland	markka
Hong Kong	Hong Kong dollar
India	Indian rupee
Israel	new shekel
Poland	zloty
Thailand	baht

Ask the children to help you to create a list of places and settings where we encounter percentages. The list will include how steep roads are, taxes, service charges, interest rates (saving and borrowing) and results of surveys.

ICT ideas *Can Do Maths* Year 6/P7 CD-ROM 3 includes 'Shopping for clothes' in which children are presented with a variety of money problems related to buying clothes. In 'Changing money' they extract information from graphs showing conversions between pounds sterling and a selection of foreign currencies including euros and Australian dollars.

Unit 10 Handling data

Term Summer 6

Framework links

6	8	112–117	Handling data	Consolidate all previous work.
		70–71	Using a calculator	Extract information from a simple frequency table and convert the data to percentages, using a calculator where appropriate.
				Interpret a simple pie chart, using fractions or percentages.
				Solve a problem by representing, extracting and interpreting data in frequency tables and bar charts with grouped discrete data.

Setting the scene

This is the final unit about handling data in Year 6/P7 and it should prove the summation of the children's learning during their primary years. During this year and in previous years, the children have had many experiences of representing and interpreting data. Through the examination, construction and interpretation of a range of graphs and charts that deal with the frequency of things, the children's knowledge and experiences are consolidated. This review and renewed exploration is then extended into the use of pie charts. The children learn how to interpret these and how to draw them. Whilst computer programs can be used to draw pie charts, we feel that to understand the principles thoroughly, it is essential for the children to have some hands-on experience of drawing.

Finally, the children are offered some charts and graphs that are either misleading or have things wrong with them. The children's evaluation of these will give a good indication of how far the children have progressed.

Starting points

The children should by now be fully familiar with block graphs, bar charts, bar line graphs and line graphs. They have all had experience of responding to these and constructing particular versions of them. The children should know how to use pairs of compasses to draw circles and how to use protractors to measure angles.

Checking progress

- All children should be able to read the charts and graphs that are presented.
- Children requiring additional support will need help with scaling and with pie chart construction.
- Some children will have progressed further and will be able to collect data, represent it and extract and interpret information from charts and graphs that they construct.

Lesson 1

Learning objectives

Mental/oral starter:
- Add several single-digit numbers

Main teaching activities:
- Extract information from a simple frequency table

Resources

Dice, an OHT of the tally chart and related story problem given below, an OHT of Resource Sheet 48, photocopies of Resource Sheet 48

Swallows	|||| |||| |||| |||
Amazons	|||| |||| |||| ||||	
Famous Five	|||| |||| ||||
Secret Seven	|||| |||| |||| |||| |||

Class 6 at Ermine St Juniors had a quiz. There were four teams.
The teacher Mrs Jewel kept a tally of correct answers.

Which team got most right?
What is the difference between the scores of the Swallows and Amazons?
How many more did the Secret Seven get than the Famous Five?

Vocabulary

Digit, add, sum, total, tally, bar chart, bar-line graph, range, grouped data

MENTAL/ORAL STARTER

Give out three normal dice to individual children. When you say "Go", each child in turn rolls their dice and calls out the number rolled. The class have to listen carefully and, after the three rolls, be able to tell you what the numbers add to. Give out another dice so that four numbers have to be added. Then make it five dice and, if appropriate, six. The children should be adding mentally as each number is called rather than trying to remember all of the numbers. You need to do the same to be able to check their answers.

MAIN ACTIVITY

Whole class, individuals

Use the OHT of the tally chart and the related story problem to revise the purpose of such charts.

Ask the children to tell you the characteristics of tally charts. Tell the class: *You know a lot about tally charts. Now I am going to give you some more charts that you should know about.*

Give out Resource Sheet 48 and ask the children to work individually to answer the questions.

■ Support
Work through the first question in each section with the children.

■ Challenge
Ask the children to devise another question for each of the charts.

PLENARY

Use the OHT of Resource Sheet 48. Discuss the fact that in the first chart the data is grouped.

Why might this have been done?

Point out that in some cases it is clearer to use a range rather than actual amounts.

For the second chart ask:

Can we join the tops of these lines to make a line graph?

Encourage the children to explain why this is not possible in this case.

Key fact or strategy

There are a variety of ways in which data can be pictorially represented.

Lesson 2

Learning objectives
Mental/oral starter:
- Add several single-digit numbers

Main teaching activities:
- Extract information from a simple frequency table
- Use percentages
- Use a calculator

Resources
Telephone directory, old bus tickets, books with ISBN numbers, calculators, photocopies of Resource Sheet 49

Vocabulary
Digit, data, percentage, grouped data

MENTAL/ORAL STARTER

Tell the children that you want them to add up the numbers that you give them. Use the phone directory, the old bus tickets, the ISBN numbers or a mixture of these to read out rows of numbers. Pause between each digit to give the children time to sum the numbers mentally. Continue as appropriate.

MAIN ACTIVITY

Whole class, pairs

Give out calculators. Use some proportions, such as 18 out of 30, 21 out of 78, 19 out of 56 and 12 out of 102, to show the children how to use the calculator to help turn these into percentages. Complete the first one by keying in $18 \div 30 \times 100 =$. This should give 60% so 18 is 60% of 30. Do the same with the next one. Here we get 26.92307. Discuss rounding with the children to get 27% (or 26.9% if you want to work to one decimal place) as the answer. Now ask them to work together on the next two. Add to the list of proportions as you wish.

Tell the children: *I am going to give you some data about passengers on a train. You will need to use percentages in this exercise.*

Give out copies of Resource Sheet 49 for pairs of children to work through.

■ Support
Work through the first example in the first question with the children.

■ Challenge
Devise an additional question to ask, based on the resource sheet data.

PLENARY

Work through the resource sheet so that different pairs of children can explain how they worked out the answers.

Key fact or strategy
Knowing the numbers in sets of a population allows you to calculate percentages. However, percentages should really be used only when you have a reasonably large number. Calling one person 25% when there are only four people in the group causes misperception about significance.

Lesson 3

Learning objectives
Mental/oral starter:
- Multiply or divide whole numbers by 10, 100 or 1000

Main teaching activities:
- Solve a problem by representing, extracting and interpreting data in a bar line graph
- Using a calculator

Resources
Calculators, photocopies of Resource Sheet 50, photocopies of General Resource Sheet D

Vocabulary
Percentages, frequency, bar line graph

MENTAL/ORAL STARTER

The children have done a lot of work on multiplying by 10, 100 and 1000 so give a few numbers for them to warm up with and then make links into place value. Do this by multiplying 10s: 10×10 is 100, $10 \times 10 \times 10$ is 1000, $10 \times 10 \times 10 \times 10$ is 10000, and so on. You can then link this to indices if you wish: $10 \times 10 = 100 = 10^2$ and $10 \times 10 \times 10 = 1000 = 10^3$, and so on. On a recent famous TV quiz programme the winning answer was to name 10^{100} – this is a googol.

MAIN ACTIVITY

Whole class, pairs

Give out calculators. Invite the children to tell you how to calculate a percentage from a proportion such as 18 out of 59. Then write 125 on the board and tell the children that this is the number of children whose work you had to mark at the weekend. Out of these 8% got full marks. How many children is that? Show the children that you need to work out $8/100$ths of 125 to get the answer. They can key this in as $8 \div 100 \times 125 =$. They should get the answer that 10 children got full marks. Try another example if necessary, say, 20% got only one question wrong.

Tell the children: *You will need to do calculations like this in the activity that I am going to give you.*

Give out copies of Resource Sheet 50 and General Resource Sheet D to pairs of children.

■ Support
Help the children with scaling the bar line graph.

■ Challenge
The children can devise another question from the information given on the resource sheet.

PLENARY

Work through the questions on the resource sheet by inviting different pairs to detail their answers and strategies. Some pairs can display the bar line graphs that they have made. Collect in the work for checking.

Key fact or strategy
Bar line graphs are particularly good for making comparisons of totals or averages.

Lesson 4

Learning objectives

Mental/oral starter:
- Multiply or divide whole numbers by 10, 100 or 1000

Main teaching activities:
- Recognise a simple pie chart
- Interpret sections on a simple pie chart
- Calculate totals on a simple pie chart
- Draw a simple pie chart

Resources
Photocopies of Resource Sheet 51, protractors (360° if they are available), rulers, sharp pencils, pairs of compasses, an OHT of the pie chart shown below

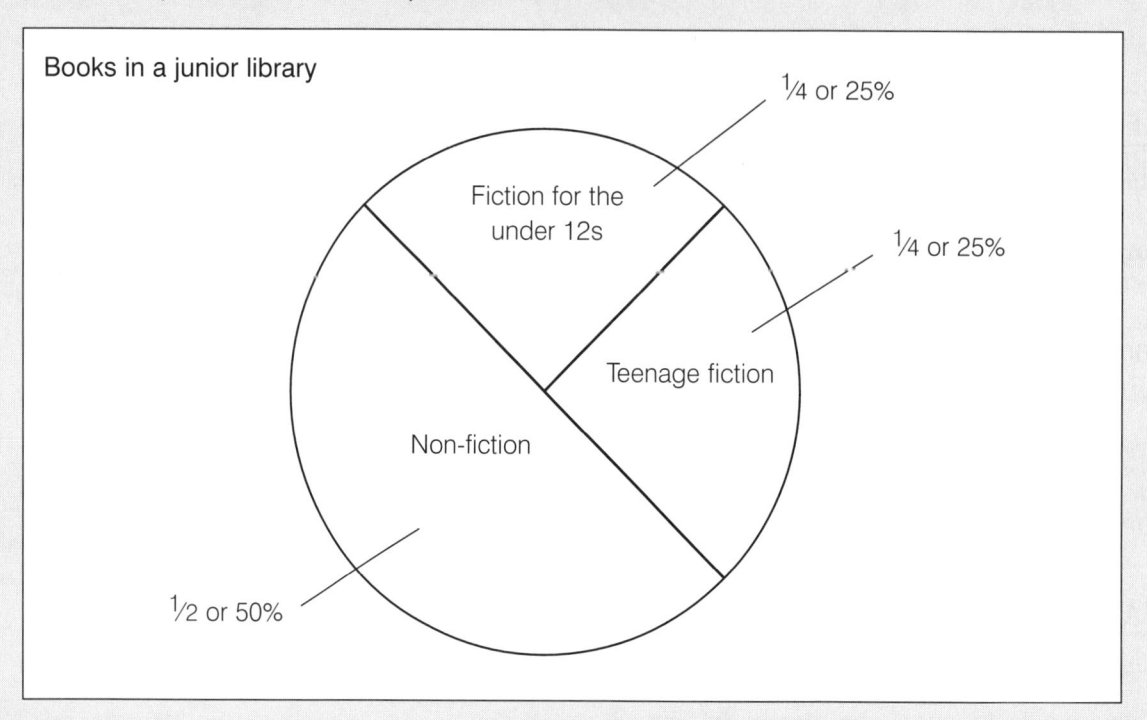

Books in a junior library

- Fiction for the under 12s — ¼ or 25%
- Teenage fiction — ¼ or 25%
- Non-fiction — ½ or 50%

Vocabulary
Pie chart, protractor, pair of compasses, sector, angle

MENTAL/ORAL STARTER

Again give a brief warm up of multiplying some whole numbers by 10, 100 and 1000. Use this opportunity to extend to decimal numbers, for example, $3.6 \times 10 = 36 \times 10 = 360 \times 10 = 3600$ and $0.48 \times 100 = 48 \times 100 = 4800$, and so on.

MAIN ACTIVITY

Whole class, individuals

Write "Pie chart" on the board. Tell the children that they are going to study these today and for the next few lessons. Use the OHT that you have prepared to stimulate discussion on how pie charts represent information. When the chart has been interpreted, draw a circle and show how we can use a protractor to measure the angles that are needed for each of the sectors. Impress on the children the fact that the fraction of the circle equates to the same fraction of the total data. Give copies of Resource Sheet 51, protractors and sharp pencils to each child. Ask the children to try to draw the three sectors. Remind them that they will have to think about what fractions the percentages represent.

When this has been done display the work of several children and review how to do the exercise. Give out pairs of compasses, with suitable warnings about safety, and ask the children to attempt the second exercise.

■ **Support**
Draw circles with the children and demonstrate angle measurement again.

■ **Challenge**
Ask the children to draw a pie chart with three sectors, one of which is ⅗ of the chart and the others ⅕ each.

PLENARY

Display some of the children's work. Tell the children that drawing pie charts is not easy so if they have managed this they have done well. Go over the drawing of a pie chart once more. Emphasise the relationship between the angle and the proportion.

> **Key fact or strategy**
> The angles at the centre of a pie chart represent the relative proportion of each sector, that is, the proportions in the data are turned into fractions of 360°.

Lesson 5

Learning objectives
Mental/oral starter:
- Convert between km and mm, kg and g, litres and millilitres, hours, minutes and seconds

Main teaching activities:
- Recognise a simple pie chart
- Interpret sections on a simple pie chart
- Calculate totals represented on a pie chart
- Calculate values on a pie chart as a percentage

Resources
Photocopies of Resource Sheet 52, calculators (for checking), an OHT of the pie chart shown below

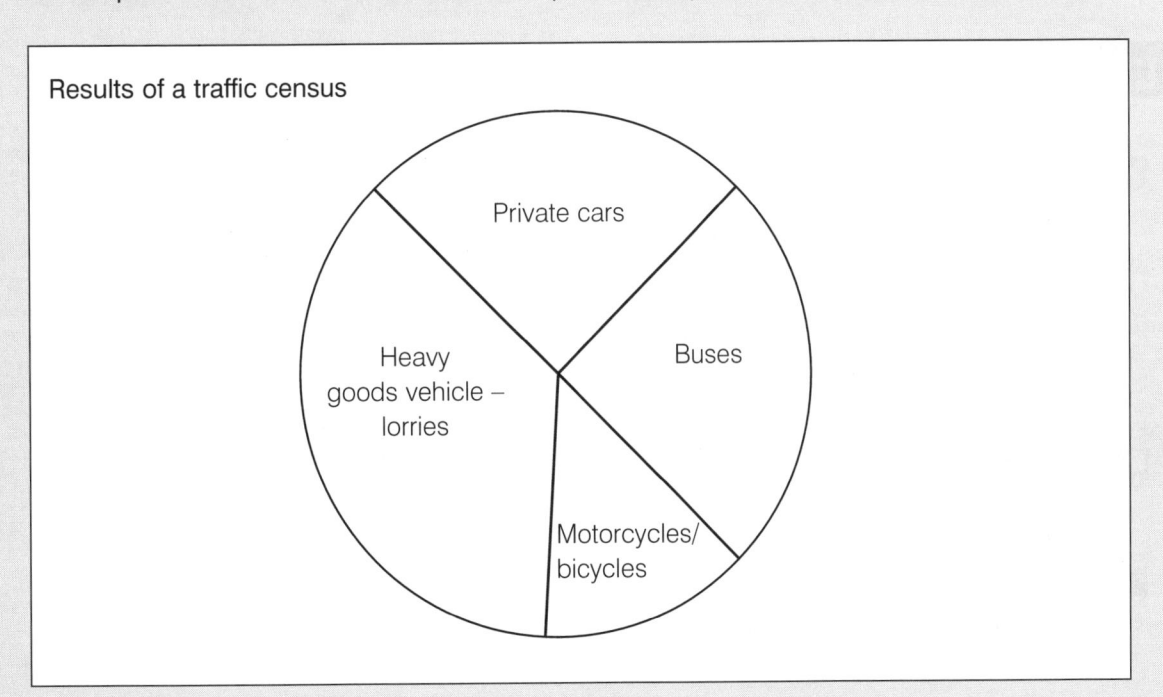

Results of a traffic census

(Pie chart with sectors: Private cars, Buses, Motorcycles/bicycles, Heavy goods vehicle – lorries)

Vocabulary
Measures terms, time terms, pie chart, section, sector, total, value, angle, percentage, results, rotation, fractional part

MENTAL/ORAL STARTER

Tell the children: *I want you to tell me what the metric measure units are for length, weight and capacity.*

Write up the units as they are mentioned and the relationships. Ask for time units and their relationships. Ask the children to extend these from seconds, minutes and hours to days, months, years, leap years, centuries and millennia.

MAIN ACTIVITY

Whole class, individuals

Review the work that was done on pie charts in the previous lesson by focusing on the relationship between angles that determine the placing of sections or sectors.

Use the OHT of the pie chart that you have made and ask the children to tell you what fraction each section is and what that is in a percentage. Tell them: *I am going to give you another pie chart and I want you to do the same sort of thing with that as you have done with this example.*

Give each child a copy of Resource Sheet 52 to work through on their own.

- **Support**

Work through the first question on the resource sheet with the children.

- **Challenge**

Ask the children to sketch a pie chart based on some colours in the classroom, for example, shoes, books, sugar paper, art materials.

PLENARY

Ask the children how they went about getting answers to the questions. As ideas and concerns emerge, deal with them through direct instruction about, for example, fractional parts and the relationship with angle divisions within a complete rotation.

Collect in the work for marking.

Key fact or strategy

Because pie charts are based upon fractions of a population they are ideal for use with percentages which are fractions of a hundred.

Lesson 6

Learning objectives
Mental/oral starter:
- Convert between km and mm, kg and g, litres and millilitres, hours, minutes and seconds

Main teaching activities:
- Recognise a simple pie chart
- Interpret sections on a simple pie chart
- Calculate totals represented on a pie chart
- Calculate values on a pie chart as a fraction or percentage

Resources
A large clock or clockface on which the hands can be rotated, photocopies of Resource Sheet 53, an OHT of Resource Sheet 53, protractors, sharp pencils, rulers

Vocabulary
Time terms, pie chart, fraction, percentage

MENTAL/ORAL STARTER

Concentrate on time in this session. There is a clear relationship between the hands of a clock and the divisions marked around the clock and the pie chart work that the children are doing. Use the hands on a clock to review one complete rotation of the hour hand (12 hours), one complete rotation of the minute hand (an hour) and one complete rotation of the second hand (a minute). Ask the children to tell you what fraction of the clock face the hour hand has moved in three hours – can they tell you the percentage? Ask what fraction the minute hand has moved in 45 seconds – can they give you a percentage? Finally, ask what fraction of the clock face the second hand has moved in 40 seconds – and again can they give you a percentage? If there is the opportunity, do this for some other amounts of time.

MAIN ACTIVITY

Whole class, pairs

Give copies of Resource Sheet 53 to each child but organise the children to work in pairs. Discuss the basic information at the top of the sheet with the whole class. All the sections are equal so the children should be able to tell you the fraction and percentage for the sections. Now tell them that people sometimes change their minds about what they would like to eat and the two exercises on the sheet are about such changes of habit.

Can you draw me pie charts for the changes?

Give out protractors, sharp pencils and rulers.

■ Support
Work through the first challenge orally and, if necessary, help the children to start to draw the pie chart.

■ Challenge
The children can invent another similar pie chart based upon a delicatessen. They could include sales of rice salad, pasta salad, chicken tikka, salami bagel, and so on.

PLENARY

Use the OHT of Resource Sheet 53 to demonstrate, with the help of the children, how to tackle the two problems. If there are errors that the children have made then discuss why these might have arisen.

> **Key fact or strategy**
> Accurate measurement of angles is essential in the drawing of pie charts.

Lesson 7

■ Learning objectives
Mental/oral starter:
- Multiply any two-digit number by a one-digit number

Main teaching activities:
- Solve a problem by representing, extracting and interpreting data on a pie chart

■ Resources
Photocopies of Resource Sheet 54 (If possible distribute these before the lesson so that the children can use them for a survey.), photocopies of General Resource Sheet E, coloured pencils, sharp pencils, rulers, protractors

■ Vocabulary
Pie chart, survey, data, logo

MENTAL/ORAL STARTER

Ask the children to tell you what the product is if you multiply each of these numbers: 26, 78, 33, 59, 42 and 91 by 2, 7, 5 and 9. Now repeat the activity by using 2.6, 7.8, and so on. Ask:

What is the product if I multiplied by 2?

Discuss how we can use what is already known from the first multiplications. Then ask for some more two-digit decimal numbers. Tell the class what each one has to be multiplied by. Finish by giving some two-digit decimals such as 0.15, 0.64 and 0.33.

MAIN ACTIVITY

Whole class, pairs or small groups, individuals

The intention in this lesson is to draw a pie chart based upon data that the children have collected. Resource Sheet 54 is a set of six logos being considered by Mr Kipper. He wants to know which of them the public most like. The children should collect data from each other and, if possible, others in the school. If the data collection can take place before the lesson that would be helpful as the sample size might then be larger than the class. Each group might be allowed to visit one class and then all results can be pooled, with your help. The children should work out how to collect and record the data.

When the data is available, remind the children about how to draw a pie chart. Encourage each child to try producing the chart. General Resource Sheet E can be used. The data should be turned into percentages or fractions in order to calculate the angle for each section or sector.

■ **Support**
Help the children to work out the proportions/percentages for a group's survey results.

■ **Challenge**
Ask the children to work with a partner to determine a list of questions for research and presentation that may interest Mr Kipper once he has his logo.

PLENARY

Display some of the pie charts. Which is the most popular logo? What difficulties did anyone have in turning the information into a pie chart? Collect in charts to form part of a wall display along with the logos.

> **Key fact or strategy**
> Pie charts are good ways of showing people's preferences.

Lesson 8

Learning objectives
Mental/oral starter:
- Multiply a two-digit number by a one-digit number

Main teaching activities:
- Consolidate previous work on frequency tables and pie charts

Resources
Photocopies of Resource Sheets 55 and 56

Vocabulary
Bar chart, bar line graph, line graph, pie chart, axis, axes, scale, division, sector, section, label

MENTAL/ORAL STARTER

Give a short test of about ten number sentences. Allow the children to mark the answers themselves. Discuss any problems. Here is an example set of number sentences.

$4.3 \times 5 =$ $6.7 \times 4 =$ $0.32 \times 6 =$
$5.5 \times 9 =$ $2.7 \times 7 =$

$0.15 \times 8 =$ $0.66 \times 3 =$ $8.2 \times 5 =$
$0.74 \times 3 =$ $0.91 \times 9 =$

MAIN ACTIVITY

Individuals, whole class, pairs

Give out copies of Resource Sheet 55 for the children to quickly fill in individually. Use the responses as the basis for a discussion of terms detailed in the resource sheet.

Give out copies of Resource Sheet 56 to pairs of children. Tell the children that there are a number of problems or errors in the charts and graphs shown.

Can you work out what is wrong?

■ **Support**
Work through the first chart with the children to indicate the sorts of things that they need to look for.

■ **Challenge**
The children can draw one of the charts correctly.

PLENARY

Go through Resource Sheet 56 and ask different pairs of children for their views about what is wrong. The mistakes are:

1 width of bars

2 odd numbers being treated vertically rather than horizontally

3 not continuous data

4 no label for the whole chart, no label for large sector, no number for total stock so only % can be calculated

5 length of line confusing, symbols not consistent

6 unsuitable treatment of the data – this data does not have meaning as a total.

Key fact or strategy
Real care needs to be taken when using pictorial representations.

Supplementary activities

Mental/oral follow-up

Give the children opportunities to try out the addition of single digits with one another. The telephone directory or ISBN numbers can be the source for the digits. Let the children find some really big numbers that are in use, for example, the distances between planets. Let them tell the class about what they find.

Ask some children to research historical measures of length or capacity, for example, furlongs, chains and the origins of the inch, or gallons and pints. Give time for them to share the research findings with the class. Relate the work done in these lessons to other mental/oral work on fractions, decimals and percentages.

Homework

Arrange for the children to develop and conduct a survey that they devise. The results should be displayed in a variety of ways that can then be discussed for appropriateness and usefulness. Resource Sheet 57 is provided to help stimulate this work.

Development

Ask the children to collect as many newspaper and magazine pictorial representations of data as they can. Get the children to examine all these in order to extract information. Use this information to discuss interpretations and, importantly, any misuses of charts and graphs. Collate outcomes of the homework exercise represented in a variety of ways. Discuss these in respect of appropriateness and usefulness.

ICT ideas

In Year 6, the *Framework for Teaching Mathematics* asks children to "begin to interpret simple pie charts, such as 'those showing the data in a computer database".

Some commercial database programs such as *Granada Database* include some prepared databases. Children could use these to graph one field against another. Alternatively, you might prepare a central database of information from one of the resource sheet exercises or another whole-class survey such as a simple questionnaire of likes and dislikes. The results of the survey could be transferred by each member of the class into the database. Children then display their results and answer specific questions using the graphing (pie chart) facility.

Unit 11 Measures

Term Summer 8–10

Framework links

8–10	15	102–111	Shape and space	Recognise where shape will be after reflection in a line not parallel to a side or in two mirrors at 90°.
				Consolidate work on translations and rotations.
		76–81	Reasoning about shapes	Make and investigate a general statement about shapes.
		86–101	Measures, including problems	Use, read and write metric units of capacity, including abbreviations.
				Know and use the relationships between them.
				Convert larger to smaller units of capacity, and vice versa.
				Know approximate metric equivalents for pint and gallon.
				Suggest suitable units and equipment to estimate or measure capacity.
				Read measurements from scales.
				Use all four operations to solve measurement word problems, including time.
				Choose appropriate operations/calculation methods. Explain working.

Setting the scene This unit completes the work on measures problems this year. Previously the children have worked on length and weight. Here they complete the set of everyday measures through solving problems about capacity. The unit further develops work on time and focuses particularly on world time zones. This work can be conveniently associated with some science and geography.

Starting points The children should be able to measure to a good degree of accuracy and understand why this is important. They will know that we use time in different ways such as timing the duration of an event and telling the time of day. They will also be experienced in calculating time taken from such things as timetables.

Checking progress
- All children should be able to read linear scales and repeating linear scales such as the markings on a clock.
- Children requiring additional support will need help with the three-dimensional quality of capacity and volume.
- Some children will have progressed further and will be able to explain why there are different time zones.

Lesson 1

Learning objectives

Mental/oral starter:
- Derive sums and differences

Main teaching activities:
- Use all four operations to solve measurement word problems
- Choose appropriate operations/calculation methods
- Explain working

Resources
Measuring jugs, cylinders and containers (for demonstration purposes), photocopies of Resource Sheet 58, calculators

Vocabulary
Digit, sum, difference, capacity, litre, millilitre, pints, fluid ounces, convert, conversion

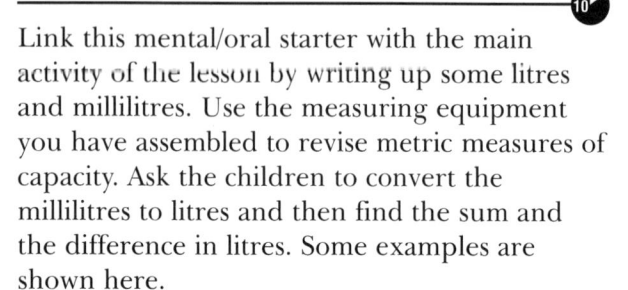

MENTAL/ORAL STARTER

Link this mental/oral starter with the main activity of the lesson by writing up some litres and millilitres. Use the measuring equipment you have assembled to revise metric measures of capacity. Ask the children to convert the millilitres to litres and then find the sum and the difference in litres. Some examples are shown here.

Sums and differences

2.6 l + 1200 ml	2.6 l – 1200 ml
8.8 l + 4500 ml	8.8 l – 4500 ml
6.9 l + 3900 ml	6.9 l – 3900 ml
3.2 l + 1800 ml	3.2 l – 1800 ml
9.5 l + 6800 ml	9.5 l – 6800 ml

When the children have done this, choose one or two of the questions and ask:

What would be the answer if there were ten times the amount in each case?

What would be the answer if there was one tenth of the amount in each case?

MAIN ACTIVITY

Whole class, pairs

Start by telling the class that pints are sometimes used in capacity, for example, in cooking. Tell the children: *There is an important fact that we need to know when using pints like this – there are 20 fluid ounces in a pint. A fluid ounce is an old measure of capacity.*

Give out copies of Resource Sheet 58. Organise the children to work in pairs to solve the problems. Make calculators available for checking purposes.

■ **Support**
With the children, work through the first question about milk and cream in Section A.

■ **Challenge**
The children can estimate how many crates of milk are carried on a milk float. How many pints and litres is this? How many gallons?

PLENARY

Work through the resource sheet step by step. Invite different pairs to help you. Ask the children to show you their calculations. Discuss any arithmetical errors with the class and analyse why these might have happened.

Key fact or strategy
It is important to make sure that you are clear about which units you are working in.

Lesson 2

Learning objectives
Mental/oral starter:
- Derive sums and differences

Main teaching activities:
- Use all four operations to solve measurement word problems
- Choose appropriate operations/calculation methods
- Explain working

Resources
Photocopies of Resource Sheet 59, calculators

Vocabulary
Digit, sum, difference, capacity, litre, millilitre, pints, fluid ounces, convert, conversion

MENTAL/ORAL STARTER

Continue with a similar exercise to the one in the previous lesson. Start to extend the challenges to three digits plus or minus two digits. Some examples are shown here.

More sums and differences

6.9 l ± 4300 ml
5800 ml ± 3.4 l
860 ml ± 0.251 m
1.25 l ± 300 ml
9.7 l ± 5.12 ml

Again with some of the examples ask:

What if they were ten times larger or one tenth of their value?

What if they were one hundred times larger?

MAIN ACTIVITY

Whole class, pairs

Do a short warm up by using the ideas shown here.

Capacity questions

- My car's fuel tank holds 35 litres. I go on a journey that uses $\frac{2}{5}$ of this fuel. How much do I have left in litres?
- If I do the return journey what percentage of the fuel have I used?
- Tell me how to write one thousand and ninety-six litres in numerals and symbols.

Give out copies of Resource Sheet 59 to pairs of children with this instruction: *Do Questions 1 and 2. Leave Question 3 about a baby paddling pool. We will do that together.*

Make calculators available for checking purposes. When the children are ready, obtain solutions and methods of working for both sets of questions.

■ Support
Do the first question about the fraction of the total amount with the children. Remind them how to work these out.

■ Challenge
Ask the children to invent another question for one of the two situations.

PLENARY

Do the final question on Resource Sheet 59 concerning the baby paddling pool. Invite individual children to help you to work out the answers. The class should be encouraged to check each step of the process.

Key fact or strategy
We often find capacity a difficult idea in terms of visualisation – we can be surprised by how much a container holds.

Lesson 3

Learning objectives
Mental/oral starter:
- Convert between km and mm, kg and g, litres and millilitres, hours, minutes and seconds

Main teaching activities:
- Use all four operations to solve measurement word problems, including time
- Choose appropriate operations/calculation methods
- Explain working

Resources
Photocopies of Resource Sheet 60, reference books containing geographical information, a set of world atlases

Vocabulary
Measures terms, hours, minutes, seconds, 12-hour clock, 24-hour clock, time zone

MENTAL/ORAL STARTER

Ask the children to tell you all the conversion facts that they know about units of measurement for length, weight, capacity and time. Write the essential facts on the board.

MAIN ACTIVITY

Whole class, individuals

Give out copies of Resource Sheet 60. Read aloud the text at the top of the page. Give the children five minutes to re-read it for themselves and then answer any questions they have.

Tell the children what time zones are. Allow them to use the world map to locate zones. Say each of the towns on the list here (they are marked on the children's maps).

Times at 12 noon GMT

When it is 12:00 noon GMT these are the times in some other places.

Auckland (NZ)	24:00
Berlin	13:00
Brussels	13:00
Cairo	14:00
Calcutta	17:30
Helsinki	14:00
Hong Kong	20:00
Jerusalem	14:00

Encourage the children to locate the towns and say what they think the time may be in each place when it is 12 noon in London.

Give the children time to record for themselves the time at each of the places on the map.

Support
Revise the 24-hour clock and digital time with the children.

Challenge
Ask the children to find out in which country each place is, by using the class atlases.

PLENARY

Collect in the resource sheets.

Give the children an oral test to check that they understand the following:

- time zone
- time difference
- Greenwich Mean Time
- an hour behind
- an hour ahead
- Earth's rotation
- longitude.

Key fact or strategy

The modern world has had to develop a standard system of time with time zones as measured from Greenwich in London. Depending on the longitude of a location, it will be ahead of or behind Greenwich Mean Time.

Lesson 4

Learning objectives

Mental/oral starter:
- Convert between km and mm, kg and g, litres and millilitres, hours, minutes and seconds

Main teaching activities:
- Use all four operations to solve measurement word problems, including time
- Choose appropriate operations/calculation methods
- Explain working

Resources
Photocopies of Resource Sheets 61 and 62, world atlases

Vocabulary
Measures terms, hours, minutes, seconds, 12-hour clock, 24-hour clock, time zone

MENTAL/ORAL STARTER

Play the game "My Aunt/Uncle went to the supermarket and bought a …". The response might be "… an alligator and it was 250 cm long". All the responses that the children give have to be an object and then something about its size (length, weight or volume/capacity). When responses are made ask the children to convert them into related units. With the example of 250 cm, ask:

What is that in metres?

Write prompts to each suggestion on the board as the game ought to continue, "My Aunt/Uncle went to the supermarket and bought an alligator that was 250 cm long, and a balloon that …", to which one of the children might respond "… weighed half a gram", and so on. Each time interpose a question that relates to conversion within the measure.

MAIN ACTIVITY

Whole class, pairs

Give each pair of children copies of Resource Sheets 61 and 62. Tell them about the game that they can play. The world map gives time zones. The city list below it gives times in various places when it is 12 noon in London (Greenwich). The children can cut out all the place cards and time cards from Resource Sheet 62.

Both sets of cards are shuffled and placed face down. Player 1 picks up a place and time, for example, Madrid and 5:00, and says, "I am in Madrid, it's 5 a.m." Player 2 picks up a place, for example, Rio de Janeiro. Player 2 has to say, "I am in Rio and it is …". They then work out the time in Rio when it is 5 a.m. in Madrid. Rio is four hours behind so it is 1 a.m. there. (The chart tells us that when it is 13.00 in Madrid it is 09.00 in Rio.)

The children can continue until they run out of cards. The cards may then be shuffled and played out again.

■ Support
Work through some trials of the game with the children.

■ Challenge
Ask the children to develop ideas about how the game can be improved.

PLENARY

Point out to the children that since the Earth rotates once in 24 hours, when it is approaching midnight in one place, it must be just after in another. Discuss the International Date Line.

> **Key fact or strategy**
> There are time zones that affect timetables and departure and arrival times.

Supplementary activities

Mental/oral follow-up Generate lots of two-, three- and four-digit numbers (include decimals with a variety of decimal places) and ask the children to tell you about these numbers. If they were lengths, weights or measures of capacity, what might they look like, feel like (in weight) and so on?

Homework Ask the children to find out what they can, from the library and on the internet, about British Summer Time and the International Date Line.

Development Ask the children to draw conversion graphs for litres and pints, and millilitres and fluid ounces. Discuss developments of the measures units that the children know. Extend them further and explore the history of imperial units.

Make a 24-hour time line/washing line with 12 midday at the centre. Invite the children to clip locations on to this, based on their estimation of what the time is when it is 12 midday at Greenwich. Vary this by changing the time at Greenwich.

ICT ideas There is a variety of web-sites that have information about time "Learn.com" (in collaboration with the Guardian); the Greenwich Royal Observatory site). Organise opportunities for the children to extract information about the history of timekeeping from these and similar sites.

Unit 12 "Real-life" problems

Term				Summer 11

Framework links

11	5	40–47	Mental calculation strategies (+ and −)	Use number facts and place value to add and subtract mentally.
		48–51	Pencil and paper procedures (+ and −)	Extend written methods to column addition and subtraction of numbers involving decimals.
		82–85	Money and "real-life" problems	Use all four operations to solve word problems involving money or "real life", including percentages.
		70–75	Making decisions and checking results, including using a calculator	Choose appropriate operations/calculation methods. Explain working.
				Check using sums/differences of odd/even numbers or doing the inverse calculation, including using a calculator.

Setting the scene

In this unit the opportunity is taken to offer the children a range of challenges that will enable them to demonstrate the important things that they have learned about solving "real-life" problems. The challenges mean that the children need to deploy their calculating ability, knowledge of fractions, decimals and percentages and their capacity to interpret word problems. An important part of the evidence that children understand "real-life" word problems is their ability to devise similar word problems and the unit offers this opportunity too. The unit can be viewed as an evaluation opportunity and a rounding off of the work that the children have done this year and in previous years.

Starting points

All the children have had regular and consistent experiences in attempting to solve problems in contexts that closely relate to everyday life. They have now had a lot of opportunities to develop their knowledge of common number bonds and ways in which to calculate answers by using different strategies – a combination of different methods and operations. They should all be confident about, or certainly aware of, the need to be interpreting word problems to identify the necessary mathematics.

Checking progress

- All children should be confident and capable in calculations using all four operations.
- Children requiring additional support will need some of the context of the word problems elaborated.
- Some children will have progressed further and will readily devise new questions that reflect the conditions of the given context.

Lesson 1

Learning objectives
Mental/oral starter:
- Find doubles/halves of decimals

Main teaching activities:
- Use all four operations involving "real life" including percentages
- Choose appropriate operations/calculation methods
- Explain working

Resources
Photocopies of Resource Sheet 63, calculators

Vocabulary
Double, halve, decimal, operation, average, mean, percentage, how many?

MENTAL/ORAL STARTER

Concentrate on doubling and halving odd number decimals. Start by doubling with some that end in 5, for example, double 1.5, 7.5 and 12.5. Try some that end in 25, for example, double 6.25, 0.25 and 14.25. Ask the children for strategies to halve something ending in 5, for example, 4.65. Possible strategies include knowing that a half of 0.5 is 0.25. Half of 4.66 is 2.33 and half of 4.64 is 2.32, and half way between these is 2.325 (half of 4.65 where the ending 25 corresponds with what we know about a half of 0.5).

Ask the children to suggest other decimals ending in 5 that everyone can attempt to halve.

MAIN ACTIVITY

Whole class, individuals

Tell the children: *I am going to plant up some hanging baskets to hang around my house. Each hanging basket will have three alyssums (white flowers) and six pansies (violet ones). I have 12 hanging baskets. How many alyssums do I need?*

When you have the answer ask:

What operation did you use to get the answer?

How many pansies do I need?

Explain that in this lesson the children are going to have to decide on which operations they need to solve some problems before solving them. Give out copies of Resource Sheet 63 for the children to work through individually. Make calculators available for checking purposes.

■ Support
Work through the cross-stitch problem with the children.

■ Challenge
Ask the children to devise a similar problem that needs two operations for its solution.

PLENARY

Invite individuals to help you to work through the resource sheet. For each problem ask:

What operations are needed?

How did you solve this problem?

> **Key fact or strategy**
> Solving word problems means that we have to interpret terms and phrases that indicate the operations that we need to work with and the order that we should work in.

Lesson 2

Learning objectives
Mental/oral starter:
- Find doubles/halves of decimals

Main teaching activities:
- Use all four operations involving "real life" including percentages
- Choose appropriate operations/calculation methods
- Explain working

Resources
Photocopies of Resource Sheet 64

Vocabulary
Double, halve, decimal, operation

MENTAL/ORAL STARTER

Take this opportunity to give a short test on the doubling and halving of decimals. The answers can be marked by each child exchanging papers with a partner before you work through each question with the whole class. Ask the children about the strategies that they employed. A set of test items is given here.

Doubling and halving decimals test

Double	6.7
Halve	3.2
Halve	0.5
Double	10.6
Halve	7.5
Double	4.25
Double	16.01
Halve	2.3
Double	0.35
Double	0.05

MAIN ACTIVITY

Whole class, pairs

Tell the children: *I have some problems for you. I want you to work with a partner to solve them and write down how you did so – this is very important.*

Give out copies of Resource Sheet 64. Do not allow the use of calculators at this stage.

■ Support
With the children, work through the first question a little at a time. Stop when you feel that the children can take over and complete the problem.

■ Challenge
The children can invent another similar problem. They should include the solution and at least one way of solving the problem.

PLENARY

Work through each of the three problems. Concentrate not only on the solutions but also on the ways in which we can approach such problems. Invite the children to tell you their strategies and explain alternative strategies as you go through the problems.

> **Key fact or strategy**
> Solving detailed problems requires careful reading and planning.

Lesson 3

Learning objectives
Mental/oral starter:
- Multiply or divide whole numbers by 10, 100 or 1 000

Main teaching activities:
- Use all four operations involving "real life" including percentages
- Choose appropriate operations/calculation methods
- Explain working

Resources
Photocopies of Resource Sheet 65

Vocabulary
Problem, solution, devise, challenge, puzzle, tools, estimate

MENTAL/ORAL STARTER

Write 50 000 000 on the board. Ask:

What does this make if divided by 10?

What do I get if I divide 50 000 000 by 100?

Do the same for 1 000. Ask the children to give an explanation as to what is happening to the digits in each case (they are moving to the right, in terms of place). Try this activity again for some other great big numbers. Ask the children to write some very large numbers on the board. For each number the class then has to divide it by 10, 100 and 10 000.

MAIN ACTIVITY

Whole class, pairs or small groups

Remind the children of the problems that they tackled in the last lesson. Tell them: *This time I want you to devise some problems that I have to solve.*

Give out copies of Resource Sheet 65 to pairs or small groups of children. The children work together to try to produce some interesting and challenging problems by using the ideas on the sheet. They need to check that the problems they produce really work. They also need to have solutions so that they can check your efforts.

■ Support
Go over the vocabulary employed on Resource Sheet 65. Discuss one or two possible ways of setting a problem by using one of the ideas on the resource sheet.

■ Challenge
Prepare a resource sheet containing the two or three best problems that the children in the group have devised. This sheet can then be offered to another teacher for their class.

PLENARY

Ask a sample of pairs or groups for a problem. Invite the rest of the class to help you to solve each of the problems. Discuss decisions that have to be made about operations, methods and strategies. Collect in all of the problems and write up a set for future use.

Key fact or strategy
Devising problems can be as challenging mathematically as problem solving.

Supplementary activities

Mental/oral follow-up

Give the children calculators and invite them to key in some decimals to halve and double. They should tell you and the class anything interesting that they find out. Ask the children to create decimals from fractions by using the calculator. What patterns of decimals do they see in a series such as $\frac{1}{5}$, $\frac{2}{5}$, $\frac{3}{5}$, $\frac{4}{5}$ and $\frac{5}{5}$? What if they double any of the decimals? Are there links to other fraction families?

Homework

Give out copies of Resource Sheet 66.

Development

Ask the children to create some number statements that can be used as a starting point for word problems. Get everyone to use these to devise word problems. Print the results as a resource bank of questions. If there are problems that can challenge other classes, arrange for your children to offer a session to another class so that they become the teachers.

Read the children's book *The Phantom Tollbooth* by Norton Juster to your class. In this story there are many interesting puzzles, jokes and conundrums linked to mathematical ideas.

ICT ideas

Lifeskills Time and Money (Learning and Teaching Scotland) offers a range of stimulating activities set within a townscape where children are encouraged to learn by solving puzzles and managing everyday situations. The teacher can customise the content of this package to meet the needs of individual ability levels.

Percentages Games (Sherston Software) offers five activities to support children's understanding of percentages in a supportive problem-solving context. For example, children must use their understanding of percentages of a whole to complete a pizza order.

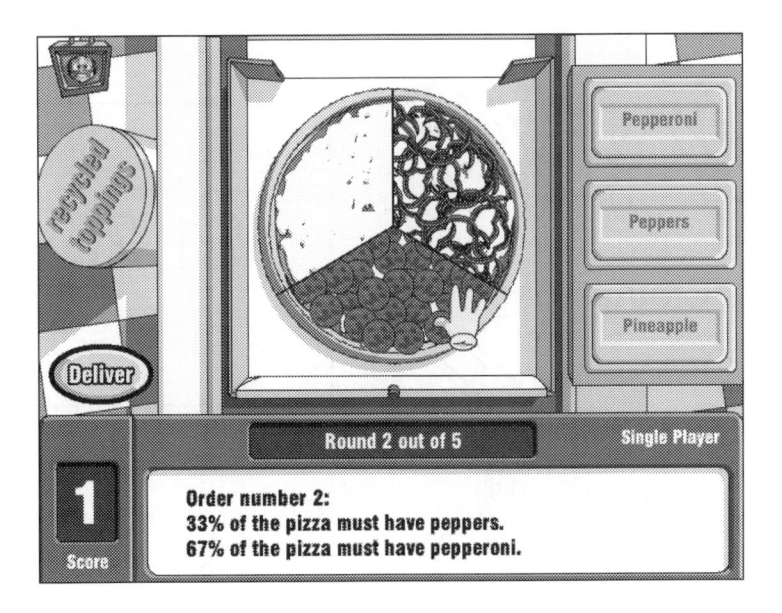

Prices

RESOURCE SHEET 1

Wooden spoon	£2.15	£2.70
Chopping board	£4.00	85p
Tea towel	76p	£1.99
	£3.65	42p
Clothes pegs	£1.25	£1.50
Sieve	90p	£5.60

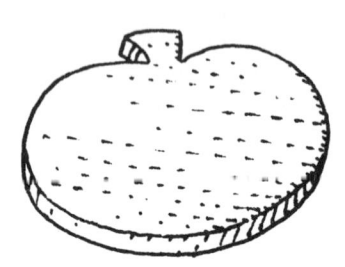

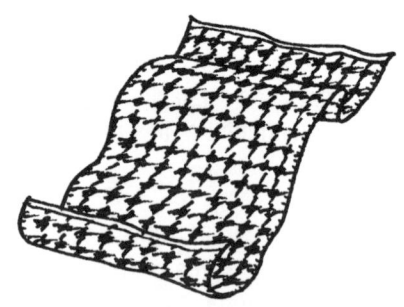

What do they cost?

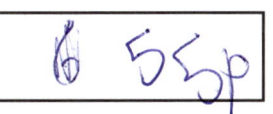

RESOURCE SHEET 2

A What is the total cost of these?

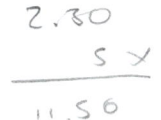

1	10	Kitchen scales	at £9.50 each	
2	5	Oval roasters	at £2.30 each	£11.50
3	100	Irons	at £17.75 each	177.50
4	70	Can openers	at £8.30 each	57.20

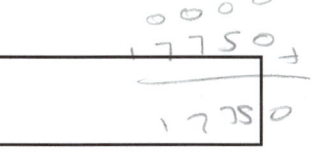

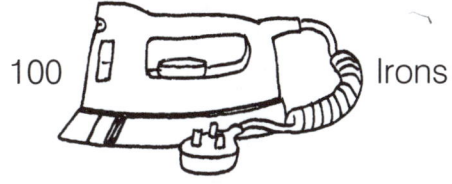

Handwritten workings:
- 2.30 × 5 = 11.50
- 17.75 × 100 = 1775.0
- 8.30 × 70 = 57.20

B What is the cost of one item here?

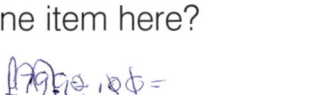

1	Cooking tool set	100 cost £799	£79.90p
2	Light bulb	70 cost £16.80	
3	Food boxes set	10 cost £88.50	£8.85
4	Pedal bin	42 cost £252.60	
5	Kitchen scissors	5 cost £11.00	55p

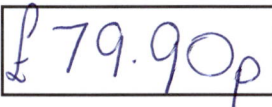

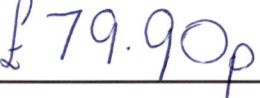

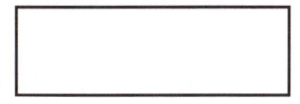

Handwritten workings: £2.50, 70×, 0.00, 15 00

Maths Action Plans, Problems and Data Year 6/P7 © David Clemson and Wendy Clemson, Nelson Thornes Ltd, 2002

Special offers

RESOURCE SHEET 3

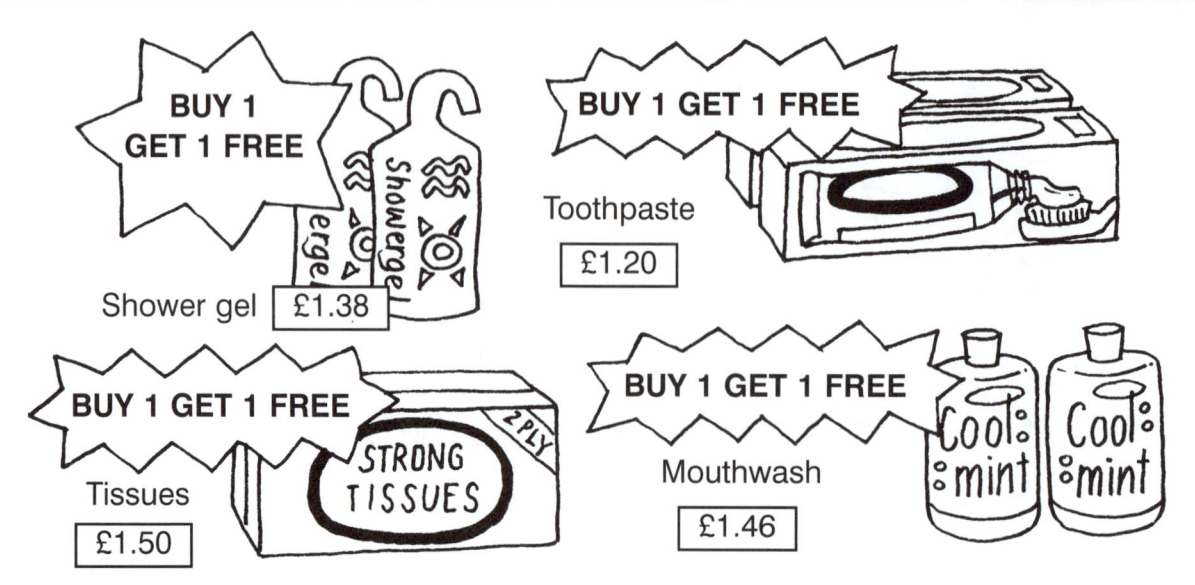

BUY 1 GET 1 FREE — Shower gel £1.38

BUY 1 GET 1 FREE — Toothpaste £1.20

BUY 1 GET 1 FREE — Tissues £1.50

BUY 1 GET 1 FREE — Mouthwash £1.46

1 Mick takes advantage of all these free offers.
What is he actually paying per item?

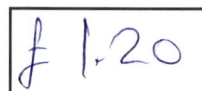

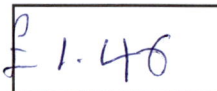

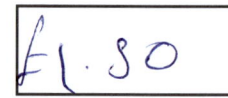

Shower gel	£1.38	Toothpaste	£1.20
Mouthwash	£1.46	Tissues	£1.50

BUY 2 GET 1 FREE — Bath foam £2.10 each

BUY 2 GET 1 FREE — Soap pack £1.80 each

2 If Mick takes 3 bath foams and 3 soap packs, what is his saving on the recommended price for each?

Saving on bath foam		Saving on soap pack	

3 Now work out the price each if the items at the top of the page were on a "BUY 1, GET ANOTHER HALF PRICE" offer (to the nearest 1p).

Shower gel		Toothpaste	
Mouthwash		Tissues	

Maths Action Plans, Problems and Data Year 6/P7 © David Clemson and Wendy Clemson, Nelson Thornes Ltd, 2002

Number bank

48	15	60	84
40	27	96	44
50	88	36	72
24	18	80	64
42	54	20	39
30	66	12	68
28	63	75	32
95	14	56	90
65	70	45	77

The music store

RESOURCE SHEET 5

Here are some of the prices in a music store.

Poster	£3.45
CD	£9.95
Cassette tape	£2.60
Blank video	£3.85

1. Wasim bought two of these items and had £3.55 change from £10.00.
   Which two did Wasim buy?

   £3.45
   £2.60

2. What would be the cost of five CDs?

   £49.75

3. If a customer bought a cassette tape and a CD, what would the change be from £20.00?

4. Melanie's change was £3.15 from £20.00.
   She bought two of one item and one other item.
   Tick the items that Melanie bought.

   1 CD   ☐   1 Blank video   ☐   1 CD   ☐
   2 Blank videos   2 Posters   2 Posters

5. Ashram has £8 to spend. What combinations of two items could he buy? What is the charge in each case?

Item 1	Item 2	Combined cost	Change from £8

A fraction of the cost

Half price

Save 1/3

Reduced in price

A What are these fractions?

1 Half of £36.18

2 Half of £950.96

3 A quarter of £96.08

4 Half of £112.00

5 A third of £36.45

Price cuts

B Some items that are being sold at half price cost these amounts. What was the original, full price?

1 £18.34

2 £106

3 £9.53

4 £257.40

5 £56.27

Bargain prices

C Some items being sold at a third off now cost these amounts. What was the original, full price?

1 £6.46

2 £58.24

3 £114.28

4 £12.50

5 £10.86

Down in prices

Stock clearance

RESOURCE SHEET 7

ELECTRICAL EXTRAS

Hurry! while stocks last

- Cassette tapes 90 — 90
- AA Battery Power — 12
- CD-R80 700 — 700
- Video VHS E-180 — 180

Write in the prices on the price tickets and how many items are in each pack. Then invent some shopping problems for a classmate to solve.

Two-digit number cards

10	11	12	13	14	15	16	17
18	19	20	21	22	23	24	25
26	27	28	29	30	31	32	33
34	35	36	37	38	39	40	41
42	43	44	45	46	47	48	49
50	51	52	53	54	55	56	57
58	59	60	61	62	63	64	65
66	67	68	69	70	71	72	73
74	75	76	77	78	79	80	81
82	83	84	85	86	87	88	89
90	91	92	93	94	95	96	97
98	99						

Three-digit number cards

620	341	117	268
796	320	990	607
402	945	932	573
232	656	467	156
910	198	879	720
745	882	121	551
376	435	760	614
527	855	290	354
810	138	262	480

Heads or tails?

RESOURCE SHEET 10

1 Make a tally of the outcomes when you toss your coin.

Throw	Heads		Tails	
	Trial 1	Trial 2	Trial 1	Trail 2
1				
2				
3				
4				
5				
6				
7				
8				
9				
10				
11				
12				
13				
14				
15				
16				
17				
18				
19				
20				
21				
22				
23				
24				
25				
26				
27				
28				
29				
30				

2 Comment on your results.

Maths Action Plans, Problems and Data Year 6/P7 © David Clemson and Wendy Clemson, Nelson Thornes Ltd, 2002

Rainfall

RESOURCE SHEET 11

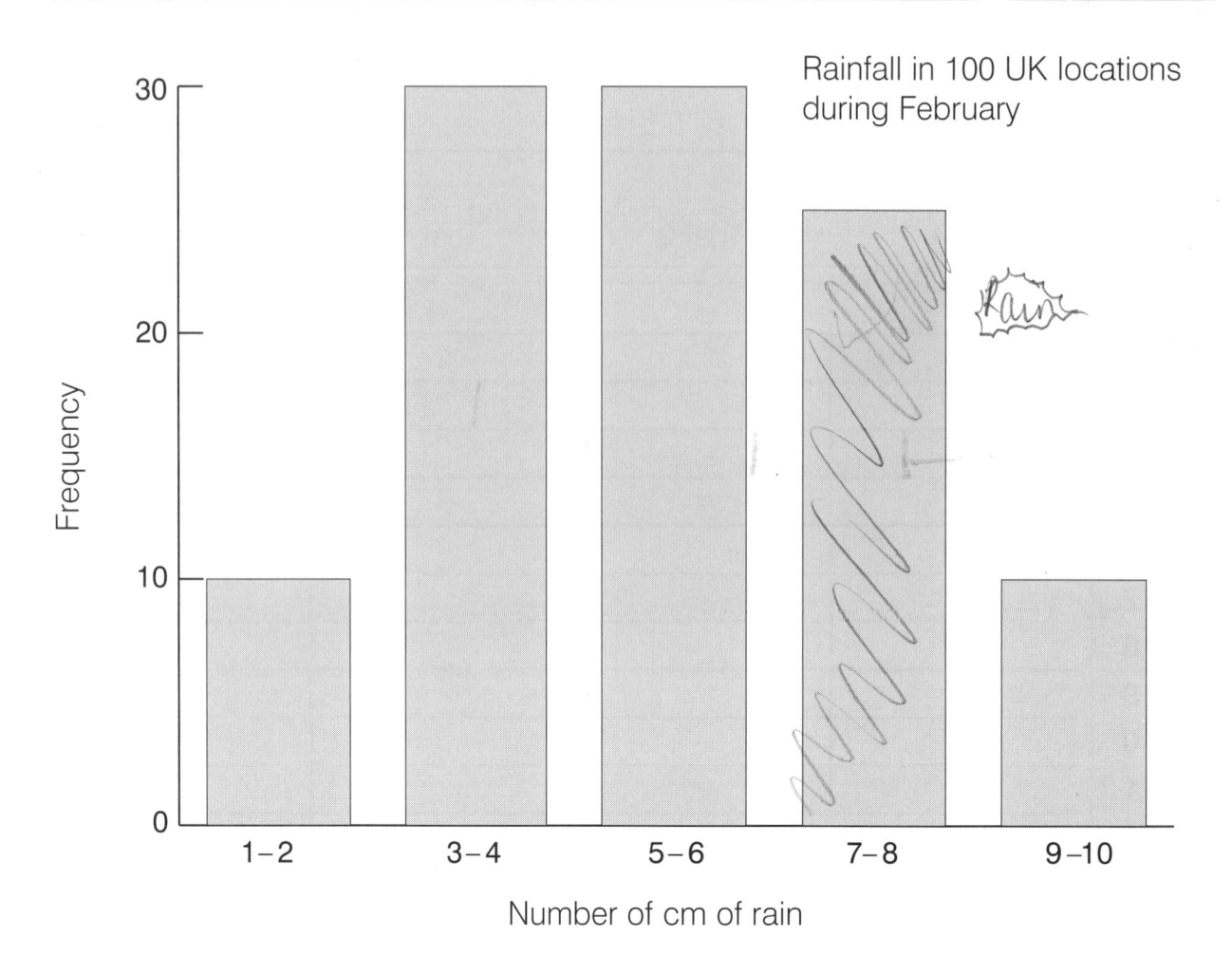

Rainfall in 100 UK locations during February

[Bar chart showing Frequency vs Number of cm of rain:
- 1–2: 10
- 3–4: 30
- 5–6: 30
- 7–8: 25
- 9–10: 10]

1 How many places reported the highest rainfall?   `2`

2 How many places had less than 5 cm of rain?   `1`

3 How can we check from the graph that 100 locations were sampled?

wrong only 95 locations were sampled

Music store

RESOURCE SHEET 12

Draw a bar chart, grouping the discrete data set out below.

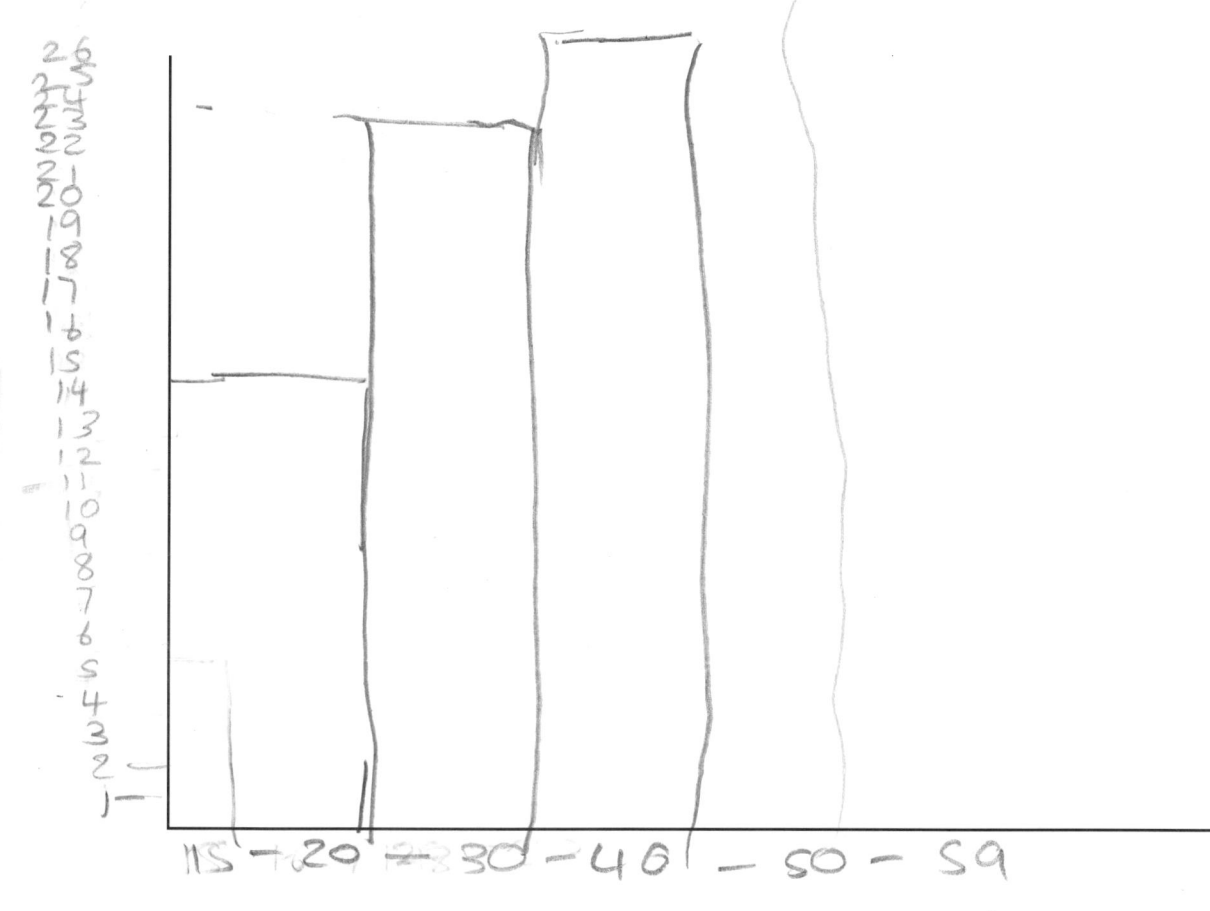

Music exam scores

5 students	15
2 students	17
7 students	20
9 students	23
14 students	27
26 students	35
18 students	42
11 students	49
5 students	54
1 student	59

Maths Action Plans, Problems and Data Year 6/P7 © David Clemson and Wendy Clemson, Nelson Thornes Ltd, 2002

The planets

RESOURCE SHEET 13

Data about the planets in the solar system

Name	Average distance from Sun (millions of km)	Circles Sun in:	
Sun	–	–	
Mercury	58	88	days
Venus	108	224	days
Earth	150	365¼	days
Mars	228	687	days
Jupiter	778	11.9	years
Saturn	1 427	29.5	years
Uranus	2 870	84	years
Neptune	4 497	164.8	years
Pluto	5 900	247.7	years

The nine planets of our system (in order from the Sun)

1. Mercury
2. Venus
3. Earth
4. Mars
5. Jupiter
6. Saturn
7. Uranus
8. Neptune
9. Pluto

Maths Action Plans, Problems and Data Year 6/P7 © David Clemson and Wendy Clemson, Nelson Thornes Ltd, 2002

Mode, median and range

RESOURCE SHEET 14

A

1 Here are the results that fifteen Y6/P7 children got out of 10 in a mathematics test.

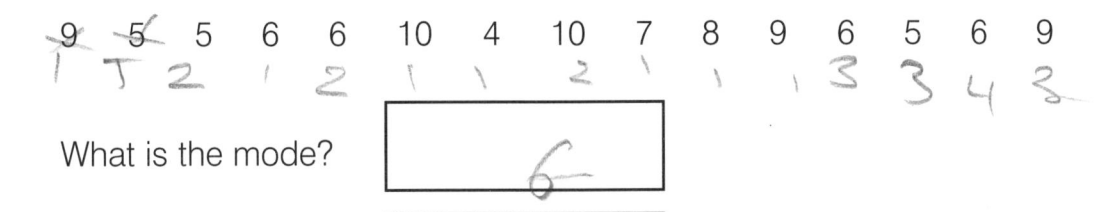

9 5 5 6 6 10 4 10 7 8 9 6 5 6 9

What is the mode? **6**

What is the range?

2 A student teacher was asked to observe the same children to see just how many minutes they were working in a mathematics lesson. The results were:

40 29 25 27 31 45 25 42 44 38 35 29 35 38 35

What is the mode?

What is the range?

B

1 The fifteen children did a science test. Here are the results:

26 32 28 29 30 28 30 26 27 26 30 30 27 28 30

What is the mode? **30**

What is the range?

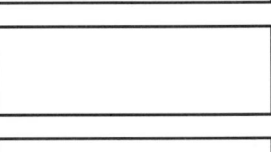

What is the median?

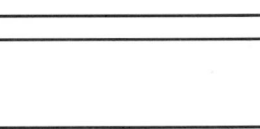

Maths Action Plans, Problems and Data Year 6/P7 © David Clemson and Wendy Clemson, Nelson Thornes Ltd, 2002

Mode, median, mean

RESOURCE SHEET 15

Here are some mathematics test results.

36	33	17	24	13	28	29
30	30	41	44	17	15	11
27	29	32	42	17	22	26
28	15	30	34	42	19	30
27	25	26	25			

Use the spaces below for your working out.

1 What is the range?

2 What is the median?

3 What is the mode?

4 What is the mean?

Throwing dice

RESOURCE SHEET 16

Throw	Outcome					
	1	2	3	4	5	6
1						✓
2					✓	
3						✓
4		✓				
5					✓	
6						✓
7					✓	
8	✓					
9		✓				
10		✓				
11			✓			
12					✓	
13		✓				
14				✓		
15				✓		
16		✓				
17		✓				
18		✓				
19					✓	
20	✓					
21			✓			
22	✓					
23						✓
24	✓					
25				✓		
26			✓			
27			✓			
28	✓					
29			✓			
30						✓

Comment on your results.

Equally likely outcomes

RESOURCE SHEET 17

A Each of these events has two equally likely outcomes. What are they?

	Outcome A	**Outcome B**
1 Tossing a coin		
2 Throwing a dice		
3 Taking a card from a full pack		

B Are these examples of events with two equally likely outcomes? Discuss some with your partner and write down what you think.

1 The current month of the year has a letter "a" in its name.

2 Jelly beans are in equal numbers of two colours, the next one from the bag will be … ?

3 If we spin a five-sided spinner is the outcome 1, 2 or 3 equally likely to the outcome 4 or 5?

4 If we throw a dice is the outcome 1, 2 or 3 equally likely to the outcome 4, 5 or 6?

5 If there are cards numbered 1 to 10 in a bag and I pull out a card, is it equally likely to be an even or an odd number?

Maths Action Plans, Problems and Data Year 6/P7 © David Clemson and Wendy Clemson, Nelson Thornes Ltd, 2002

Probability

Talk about and write down what the probability is of pulling these cards from the pack.

1 A heart ♥ card   3

2 A black card ♣ ♠   6

3 A number card **2 3 4 5 6 7 8 9 10**

4 An eleven card **11**

5 A card with a number or picture on it

6 A card with a picture on it

String story problems

RESOURCE SHEET 19

Greeno
garden twine
3 m

Matto
rope for mat making
12 m

Washo
washing line
20 m

Mrs Bumble is a great one for string. She finds lots of uses for it. Help her to solve these string problems.

1. Mrs Bumble makes rope mats for a bazaar. Each mat takes 244 cm. If she cuts a length for one mat off her ball of Matto, how much is left?

2. How many mats can be made from a complete ball of Matto?

3. If 976 cm have been cut from a ball of Matto how many mats have been made?

4. Mrs Bumble tied the roses back with these lengths of Greeno: 1.02 m, 67 cm, 41 cm, 8.9 cm and 26.75 cm. How much is left on her ball of garden twine?

5. Mrs Bumble made a twine net to go over a strawberry plant. She began with a new ball of Greeno and 238 cm were left. How much twine did she use?

6. The washing line stretches 3 times across the yard. It takes 16.11 m of line. How long is each of the 3 lengths if they are all the same length?

7. Mrs Bumble's granddaughter wants a skipping rope. She needs 1.59 m of line. How much would be left from a complete roll of Washo?

8. How much Washo line is needed for 7 skipping ropes?

Maths Action Plans, Problems and Data Year 6/P7 © David Clemson and Wendy Clemson, Nelson Thornes Ltd, 2002

Multi-sport challenge

RESOURCE SHEET 20

A In a multi-sport challenge participants have to run, cycle, canoe and horse ride over a long distance. The total race covers 80.5 km. Now solve these problems.

1 The running and cycling parts of the race cover 51.8 km. Contestants run 9.75 km. How far do they have to cycle?

2 They then canoe across a lake. One fifth of the way ~~9.75 km exactly~~ across they have canoed 1.05 km. How far is it across the lake?

3 Once across the lake the rest of the race is on horseback. How far is this part of the race?

B 1 If you were asked to draw a scale diagram of the race, to fit on a piece of paper the size of this resource sheet, what unit would you use to represent a km?

2 What measuring tool(s) would you use?

C 1 Invent a multi-sport distance event of your own. Set up some challenges for your classmates to solve. Use a calculator to help you.

Maths Action Plans, Problems and Data Year 6/P7 © David Clemson and Wendy Clemson, Nelson Thornes Ltd, 2002

Time to make rugs

RESOURCE SHEET 21

A In an automated rug-making factory the time taken to make a rug is exactly related to the amount of wool needed. The manager has to complete a table which will show how quickly rugs of a range of weights can be made.
Nylon rugs can be made slightly quicker. See if you can complete his table.

	Amount of wool/nylon needed	1 kg	5 kg	7.5 kg	12 kg	15 kg
Wool	Make up time	20 mins				
Nylon	Make up time	15 mins				

B 1 During her shift Waheeda supervised one making of five wool rugs, each taking 5 kg wool. How long was her shift?

2 How long would a machine need to run to produce 16 nylon rugs, each using 12 kg raw material?

3 How many more nylon rugs of 7.5 kg than wool rugs of the same size could be made in 18¾ hours?

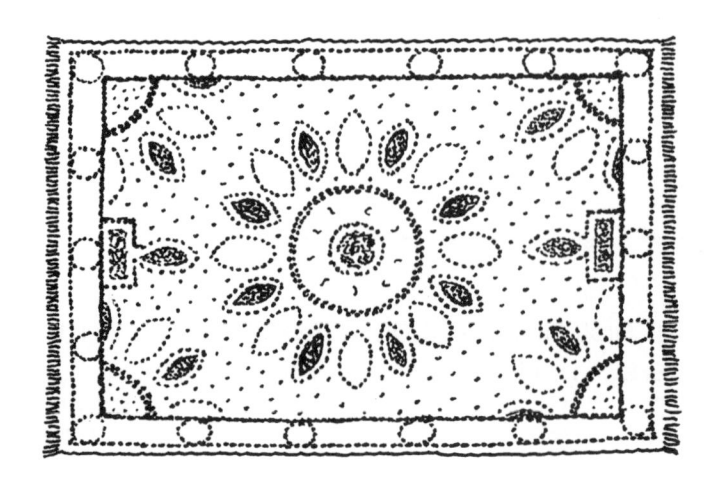

Measurement cards

RESOURCE SHEET 22

Cut out each number card

1.5 m	100 cm	0.1 m	1 mm
0.10 m	100 000 mm	200 m	50 cm
0.01 m	0.02 m	5 mm	1 m
10 m	10 m	15 cm	1.5 m
10 cm	20 mm	100 m	100 m
0.1 m	10.5 cm	2 m	0.05 m
200 cm	0.5 m	100 mm	1000 cm
10 m	1000 mm	20 m	20 cm
10 000 mm	0.2 m	0.1 cm	10.5 cm

Maths Action Plans, Problems and Data Year 6/P7 © David Clemson and Wendy Clemson, Nelson Thornes Ltd, 2002

Railway timetable

RESOURCE SHEET 23

Here are the times for two trains on the Transpennine Express.

Cleethorpes	↓ 07:15	16:55
Grimsby Town	07:23	16:46
Habrough	07:33	16:31
Barnetby	07:41	16:22
Scunthorpe	07:56	16:08
Doncaster	08:25 dep 08:27	15:40 dep 15:42
Meadowhall	08:46	15:17
Sheffield	08:54 dep 09:10	15:08 dep 15:11
Stockport	09:51	13:40
Manchester Picc.	10:04	14:19
Manchester Airport	10:31	↑ 13:56

See if you can answer these questions by consulting the timetable.

1 How long do the Transpennine journeys take in both directions?

From Cleethorpes [ ]

From Manchester Airport [ ]

2 What is the shortest time taken between stations? [ ]

What is the longest time taken between stations? [ ]

3 How long do the following journeys take?

Habrough to **Meadowhall** [ ]

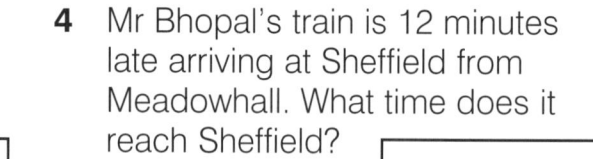

Sheffield to **Manchester Piccadilly** [ ]

Doncaster to **Barnetby** [ ]

Sheffield to **Grimsby town** [ ]

4 Mr Bhopal's train is 12 minutes late arriving at Sheffield from Meadowhall. What time does it reach Sheffield? [ ]

It loses another 7 minutes on the remainder of the journey. What time does it reach Manchester Airport? [ ]

Maths Action Plans, Problems and Data Year 6/P7 © David Clemson and Wendy Clemson, Nelson Thornes Ltd, 2002

Small measuring tools

RESOURCE SHEET 24

1 Find two very small things like a paper clip and a suitcase key.

Measure the lengths of these as exactly as you can in millimetres.
Use them as measuring tools and compare them with as many of the items below as you can. Measure the lengths or widths of the items in millimetres.

- a spent match
- a drawing pin
- a one penny coin 
- a cuff button
- a safety pin
- a cup hook

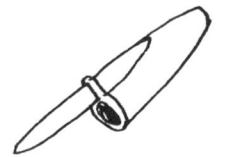

- a jelly bean
- a postage stamp 
- a staple
- a hair grip
- a pen top
- a 5p coin

2 When you have measured all these items, place them in order of length (rank order), starting with the longest.

3 Which of the things you have measured is nearest to each of the following measurements?

1 cm _____

3 cm _____

0.035 m _____

0.02 m _____

0.01 m _____

Maths Action Plans, Problems and Data Year 6/P7 © David Clemson and Wendy Clemson, Nelson Thornes Ltd, 2002

Which operation?

RESOURCE SHEET 25

You need to use two of the following operations to solve all these problems. Study the problems carefully and then tick the two operations you need to use.

Addition ☐   Subtraction ☐   Multiplication ☐   Division ☐

Then work out the problems.

---

1 Business at the Thomas Pottery Works is not going well. They have sold 4 368 fewer teacups this year than last, when 15 762 were sold. What are this year's sales of cups?

2 Kilns 1 and 2 fire 3 740 items each. How many in total can be fired in kilns 1 and 2?

3 Stocks of plates in the pottery shop vary.
   a) On Monday there are 1 230 in stock and then 741 are sold. Tuesday's new stock is 544 and 320 are sold. Here is the stock for the rest of the week.

	New	Sold	Stock
Wednesday	1293	638	
Thursday	422	502	
Friday	1011	467	
Saturday	370	1076	

Work out the stock at the end of each day. Complete the table.

   b) What number of plates needs to be delivered as new stock on the next Monday to restore last Monday's stock figure?

   c) From 10 055 plates fired in the kiln 8 742 survived. How many plates cracked or broke in the kiln?

4 Work out the sales of the Woodland and Seashore teasets from this information.

   a) 537 Woodland and 7 831 Seashore sets

   b) 1 762 Woodland and 369 fewer Seashore sets

   c) 679 more Woodland sets were sold than Seashore sets. 111 553 Seashore sets were sold. How many teasets were sold altogether?

Choose your operations

RESOURCE SHEET 26

Carefully look at each of the problems below. Decide which operations you need to solve the problems and tick the boxes, then go ahead and solve the problems.

---

1 Morris has entered a TV quiz. If he answers every question correctly, his score (which is 1 for the first question) is doubled each time. How many questions must he answer correctly to get more than 120 points? ✓

Addition ☐ Subtraction ☐
Multiplication ☐ Division ✓

2 Toy gift packs contain 3 princesses for every 1 wild wolf. One pack contains 450 princesses. How many wild wolves will there be?

Addition ☐ Subtraction ☐
Multiplication ☐ Division ☐

3 In 112 toy surprise bags 7/8 have a moving toy. Of these 3/7 are jumping beetles and the rest are creeping snakes.

a) How many have beetles?

b) How many have snakes?

c) How many have neither?

Addition ☐ Subtraction ☐
Multiplication ☐ Division ☐

4 Zak shares his badge collection among his 13 friends. He has 221 badges. How many badges should:

a) 3 friends have?

b) 8 friends have?

Addition ☐ Subtraction ☐
Multiplication ☐ Division ☐

5 I think of a number, multiply it by 3 and add 2.32. I get 25. What is the number I first thought of?

Addition ☐ Subtraction ☐
Multiplication ☐ Division ☐

Maths Action Plans, Problems and Data Year 6/P7 © David Clemson and Wendy Clemson, Nelson Thornes Ltd, 2002

Lisa's workstation

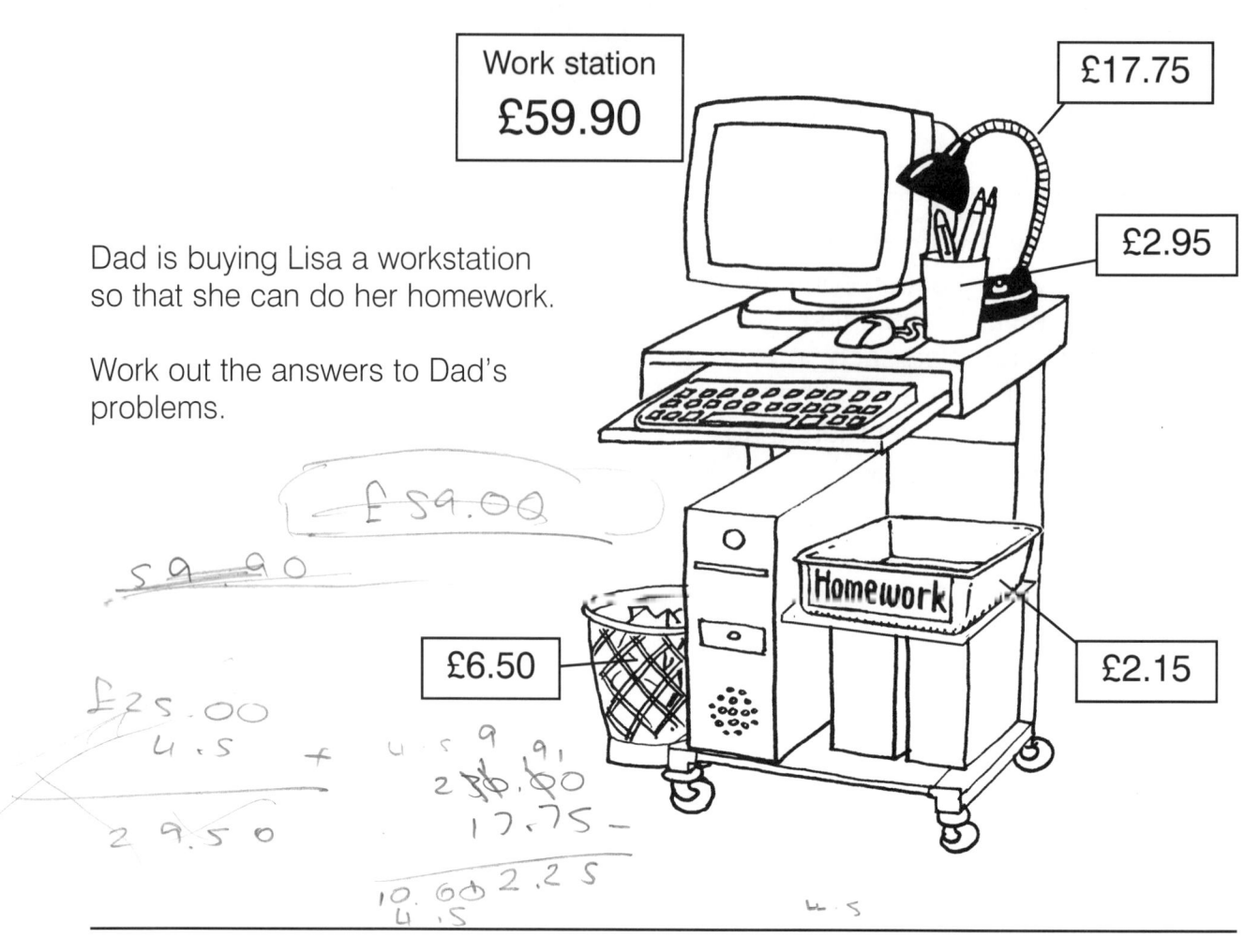

RESOURCE SHEET 27

Work station **£59.90**

£17.75

£2.95

Dad is buying Lisa a workstation so that she can do her homework.

Work out the answers to Dad's problems.

£6.50

£2.15

1 If he pays for the computer in three equal instalments, how much will each be? (It costs £499.50.)

I don't know!

2 How much change from £30 will he have for the lamp, bin, pencil pot and homework tray?

£12.25

3 He pays a £5 deposit for the workstation and then the balance in two instalments. How much is each instalment?

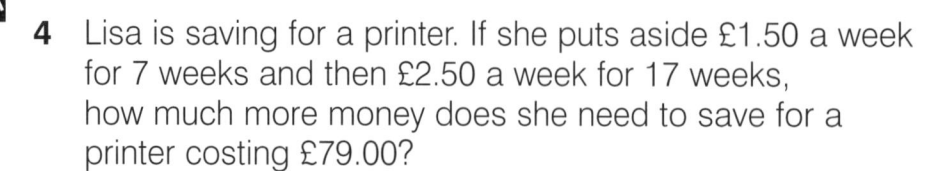

4 Lisa is saving for a printer. If she puts aside £1.50 a week for 7 weeks and then £2.50 a week for 17 weeks, how much more money does she need to save for a printer costing £79.00?

5 Computer disks are 58p each and printer cartridges £4.99. Lisa has £25. If she buys four printer cartridges how many computer disks can she also buy?

Maths Action Plans, Problems and Data Year 6/P7 © David Clemson and Wendy Clemson, Nelson Thornes Ltd, 2002

The River Festival

RESOURCE SHEET 28

Use a calculator or a written method.

1. In the summer, 3026 tickets were sold for the River Festival. Each ticket cost £7.20. What was the cost of all the tickets?

2. People who entered the raft race paid £2.55 each. The total sum taken was £698.70. How many entries were there?

3. The organisers purchased 48 ribbons and prizes for the events at 97p each. How much did they all cost?

4. Engraving the winner's name on the River Festival Cup costs about £14.50. The festival is an annual event. If engraving prices stay the same, how much should be in the budget for engraving, for the next:

   2 years?

   5 years?

   10 years?

   Use this space for your working out.

Maths Action Plans, Problems and Data Year 6/P7 © David Clemson and Wendy Clemson, Nelson Thornes Ltd, 2002

Percentage game

RESOURCE SHEET 29

You need two players, a dice, two counters, percentage cards and play money.

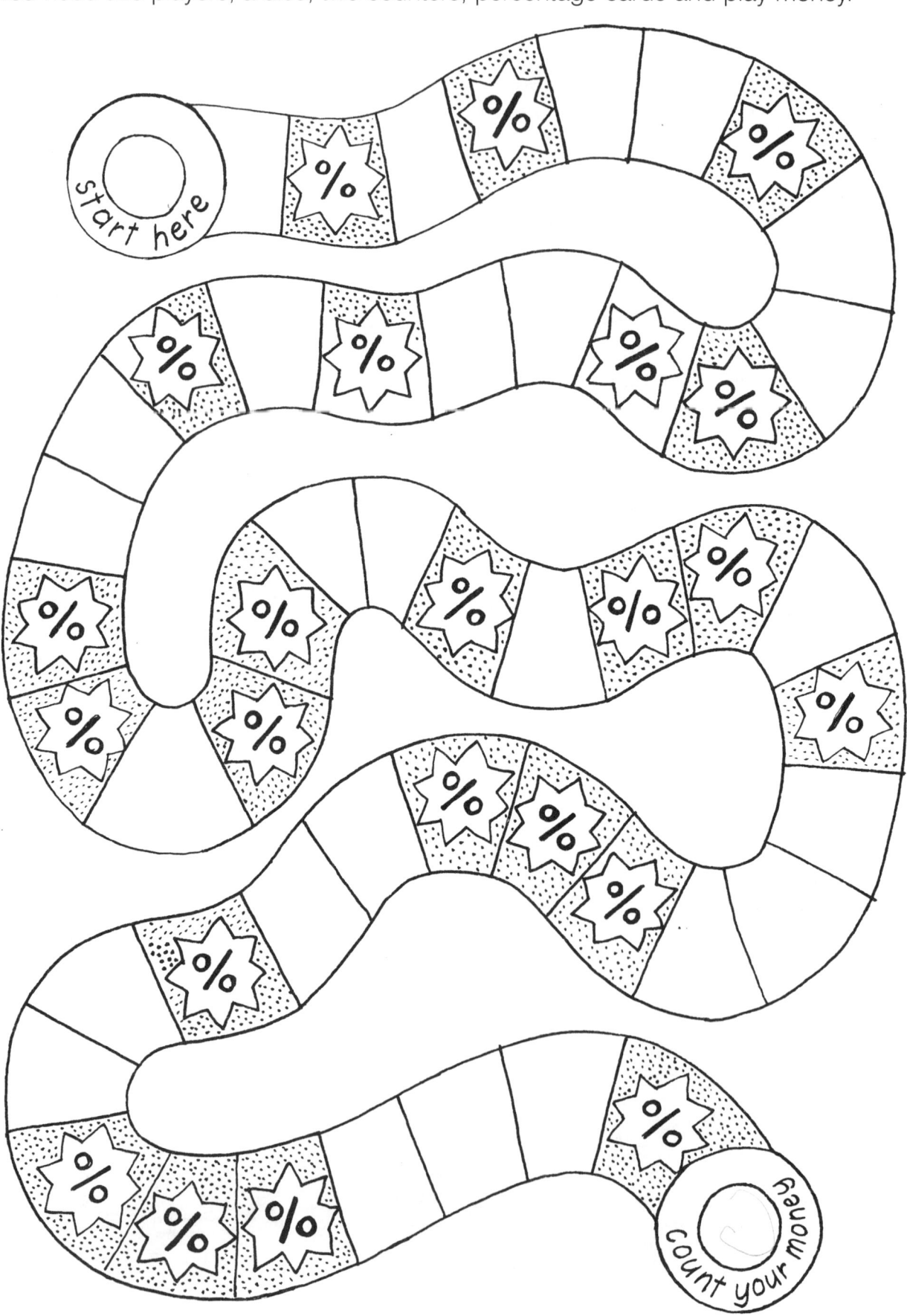

Start here ... *count your money*

Percentage game cards

RESOURCE SHEET 30

Cut out each number card.

Give opponent 100% of £10	Give bank 25% of £100	Give opponent 12% of £50	Give bank 10% of £500
Give opponent 4% of £150	Give bank 70% of £70	Give opponent 2.5% of £600	Give bank 1% of £200
Give opponent 120% of £60	Give bank 1% of £300	Give opponent 3% of £1600	Give bank 5% of £60
Give opponent 7.5% of £40	Give bank 2.5% of £400	Give opponent 2% of £350	Give bank 20% of £120

Maths Action Plans, Problems and Data Year 6/P7 © David Clemson and Wendy Clemson, Nelson Thornes Ltd, 2002

Percentage game coins

RESOURCE SHEET 31

Teen Scene's sale

RESOURCE SHEET 32

Teen Scene have a sale on. Work out the sale prices according to the discount set. These are the full prices.

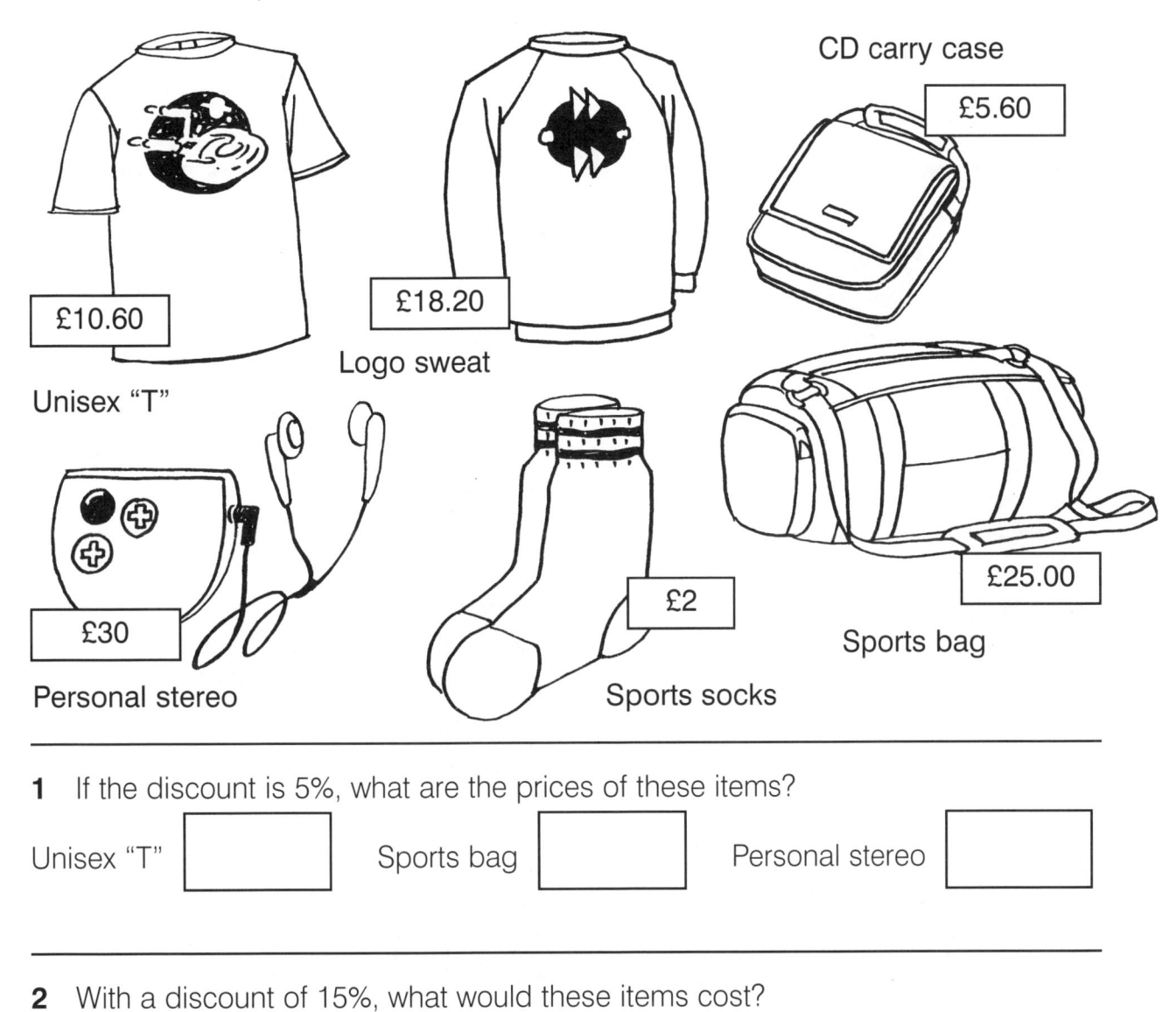

- Unisex "T" — £10.60
- Logo sweat — £18.20
- CD carry case — £5.60
- Personal stereo — £30
- Sports socks — £2
- Sports bag — £25.00

1 If the discount is 5%, what are the prices of these items?

Unisex "T" [ ]   Sports bag [ ]   Personal stereo [ ]

2 With a discount of 15%, what would these items cost?

Logo sweat [ ]   Sports socks [ ]   Unisex "T" [ ]

3 Prices are slashed by 50%. What do they all cost now?

Unisex "T" [£1.06]   Logo sweat [ ]   CD carry case [ ]

Sports socks [ ]   Sports bag [ ]   Personal stereo [ ]

Maths Action Plans, Problems and Data Year 6/P7 © David Clemson and Wendy Clemson, Nelson Thornes Ltd, 2002

Comparing weights

RESOURCE SHEET 33

HEALTH FOOD STORES
Pulses · Peas · Beans · Dried Fruits · Rice

Use a calculator if you need one.
Check your work.

1. Which is more – 1 lb or 1 kg of chick peas?

2. Which is more – 500 g or 12 oz lentils?

3. Which is less – 60 g or 1½ oz of cannelloni beans?

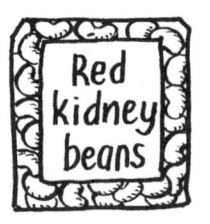

4. Which is less – 10.5 lbs or 1.05 kg red kidney beans?

5. To make up a pack of 2.5 kg apricots how many grams have to be added to 1.03 kg?

6. A pack of 1 kg is made up of 305 g, 76 g, 34 g and ... ? How many more grams?

7. 3 oz of banana chips weigh how many grams?

8. 5 kg of rice is…
how many g?
how many lb and oz?

9. How many packs of 53 g of pineapple chunks can be made up from a sack weighing 2 kg 968 g?

10. 67 packs of raisins each weigh 42 g. How much do all the packs weigh?

Maths Action Plans, Problems and Data Year 6/P7 © David Clemson and Wendy Clemson, Nelson Thornes Ltd, 2002

Recipes

A teaspoon usually holds 5 ml of liquid.
(A tablespoon holds 3 times this amount.)

Meena and Owen want to do some cooking. They have a recipe book with imperial units in it. Can you convert their recipes to metric units?

Apple flapjack

2 oz margarine
2 level tbsp golden syrup
2 oz demerara sugar
6 oz rolled oats

Filling
1 oz margarine
1 lb cooking apples
2 oz granulated sugar

Apricot sponge

6 oz margarine
6 oz Barbados sugar
3 large eggs
6 oz self-raising flour
1 tsp apricot jam

Filling
3 oz margarine
2 oz sugar
2 tbsp apricot jam

Tiger biscuits

4 oz plain flour
4 oz margarine
1 oz caster sugar
1 oz chopped walnuts

Filling
1½ oz margarine
1½ oz icing sugar
½ tsp coffee essence
2 oz almonds

Maths Action Plans, Problems and Data Year 6/P7 © David Clemson and Wendy Clemson, Nelson Thornes Ltd, 2002

Measuring tools at home

RESOURCE SHEET 35

Look around your home to find tools for measuring length, mass or volume. Fill in the chart below.

Name of tool	What we use it for	Units of measurement it displays

Distance conversion graph

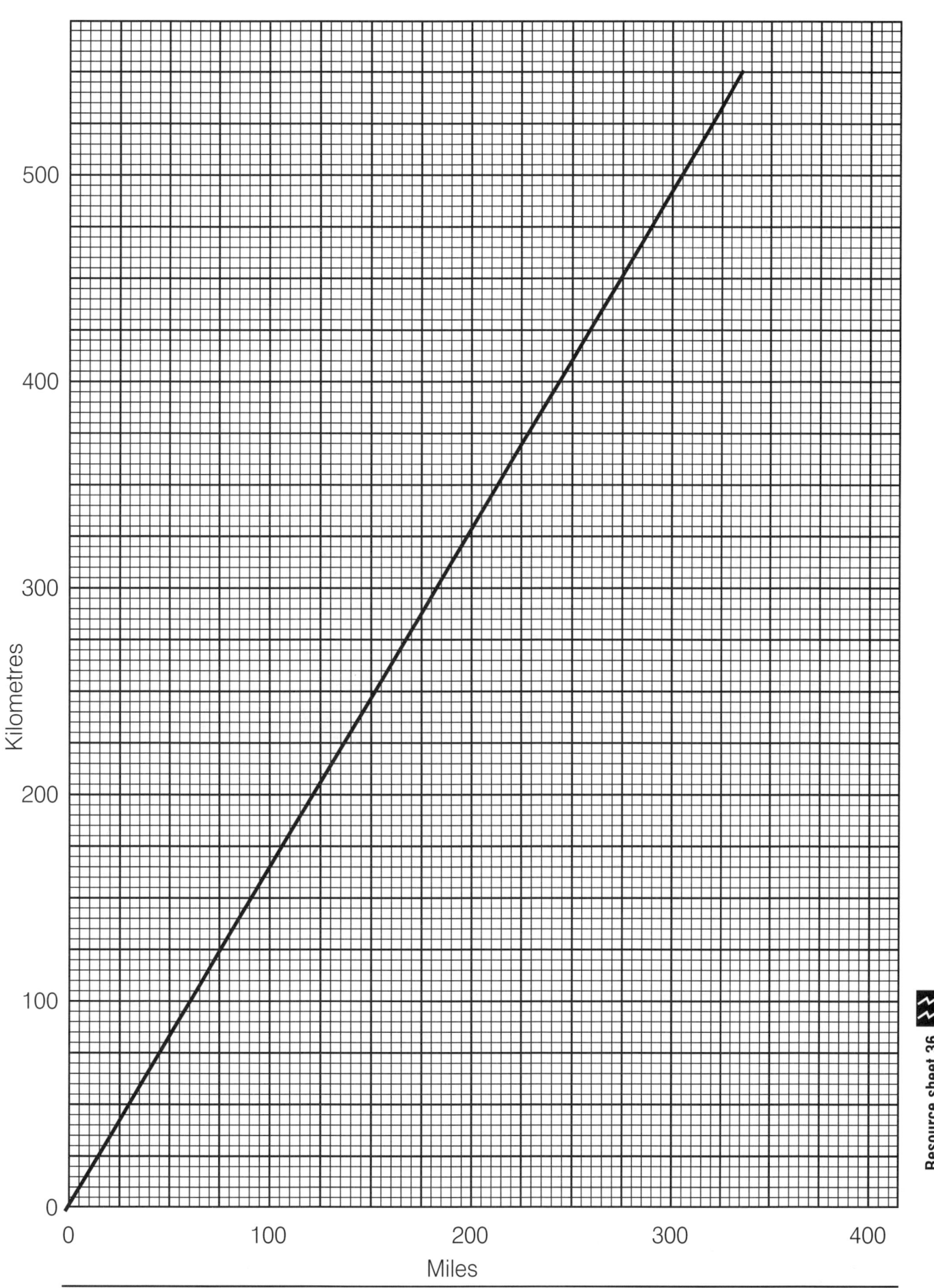

RESOURCE SHEET 36

Mileage chart

Hull	Kendal	Leeds	Lincoln	Middlesborough	Nottingham	Sheffield	York
165							
61	74						
47	177	73					
89	82	64	125				
153	203	73	36	131			
67	121	35	48	104	44		
38	90	24	81	50	87	60	

Temperature graph

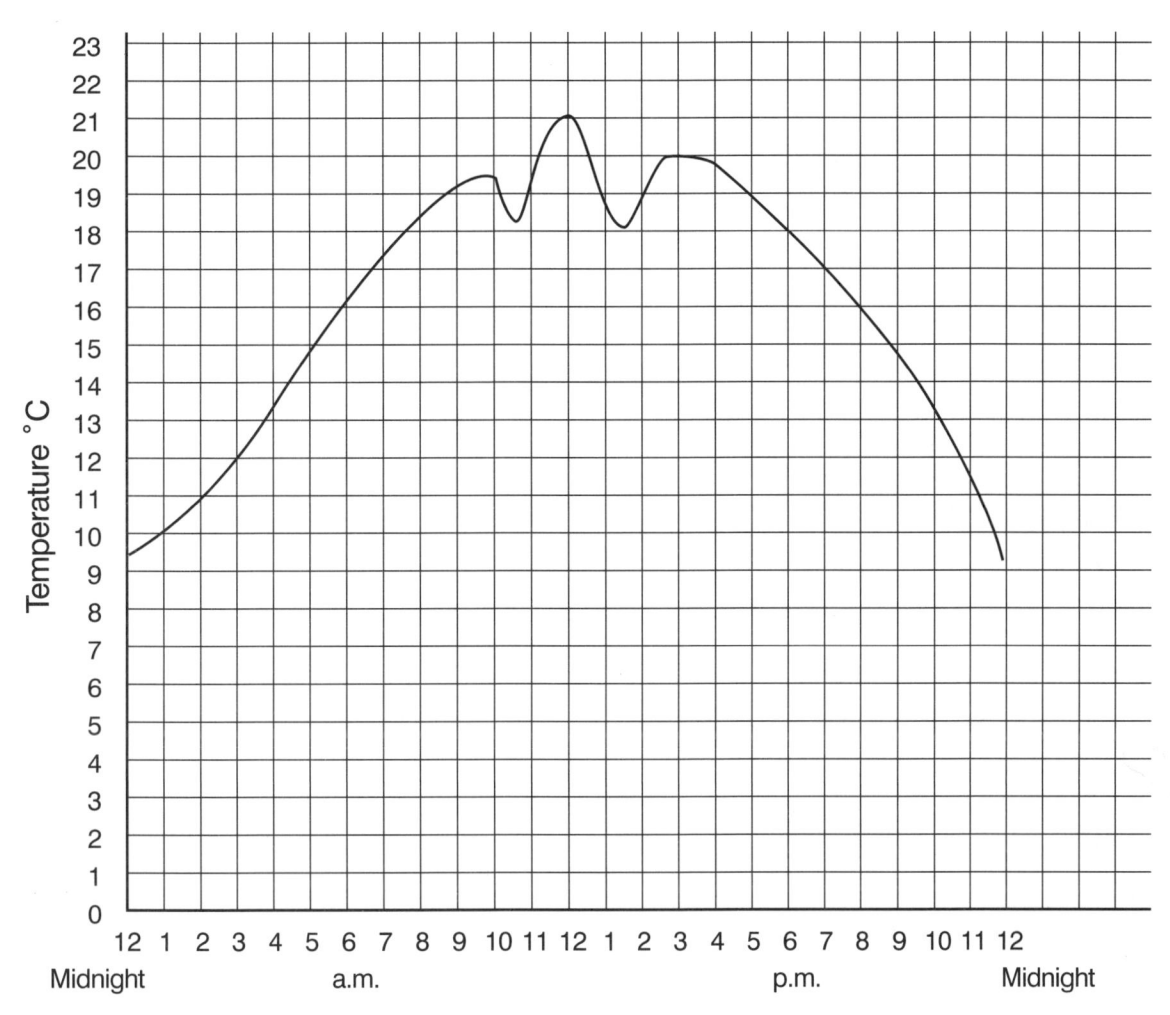

RESOURCE SHEET 38

A temperature sensor was put inside a classroom door and connected to a computer so that temperature readings were recorded every hour through one day and one night (24 hours).

1. What was the coolest temperature? — 9°C

   When did this occur? — 12 am

2. When was it warmest?

3. What do you think happened at 10.15 a.m.?

   What happens on the graph at this time?

4. What was the maximum classroom temperature?

5. Why did the classroom temperature start to drop between 3 p.m. and 4 p.m.?

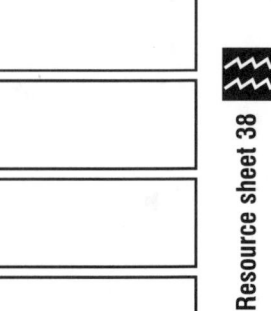

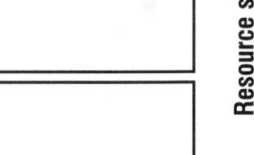

A journey

Here is the data to put on a distance–time graph.

Time	Distance travelled/km
10:00	0
10:30	25
11:00	45
11:30	70
12:00	90
12:30	90
1:00	90
1:30	120
2:00	145
2:30	170
3:00	185
3:30	200
4:00	200

Draw in the graph of the car journey and then answer these questions.

1 How far did the car travel in the total time of six hours?

2 How far had the car gone two hours after departure?

3 What might have happened between 12 noon and 1 p.m.?

4 About what time did the journey end?

5 How long did the journey take?

6 What might have happened between 2 p.m. and 2.30 p.m.?

Temperature conversion

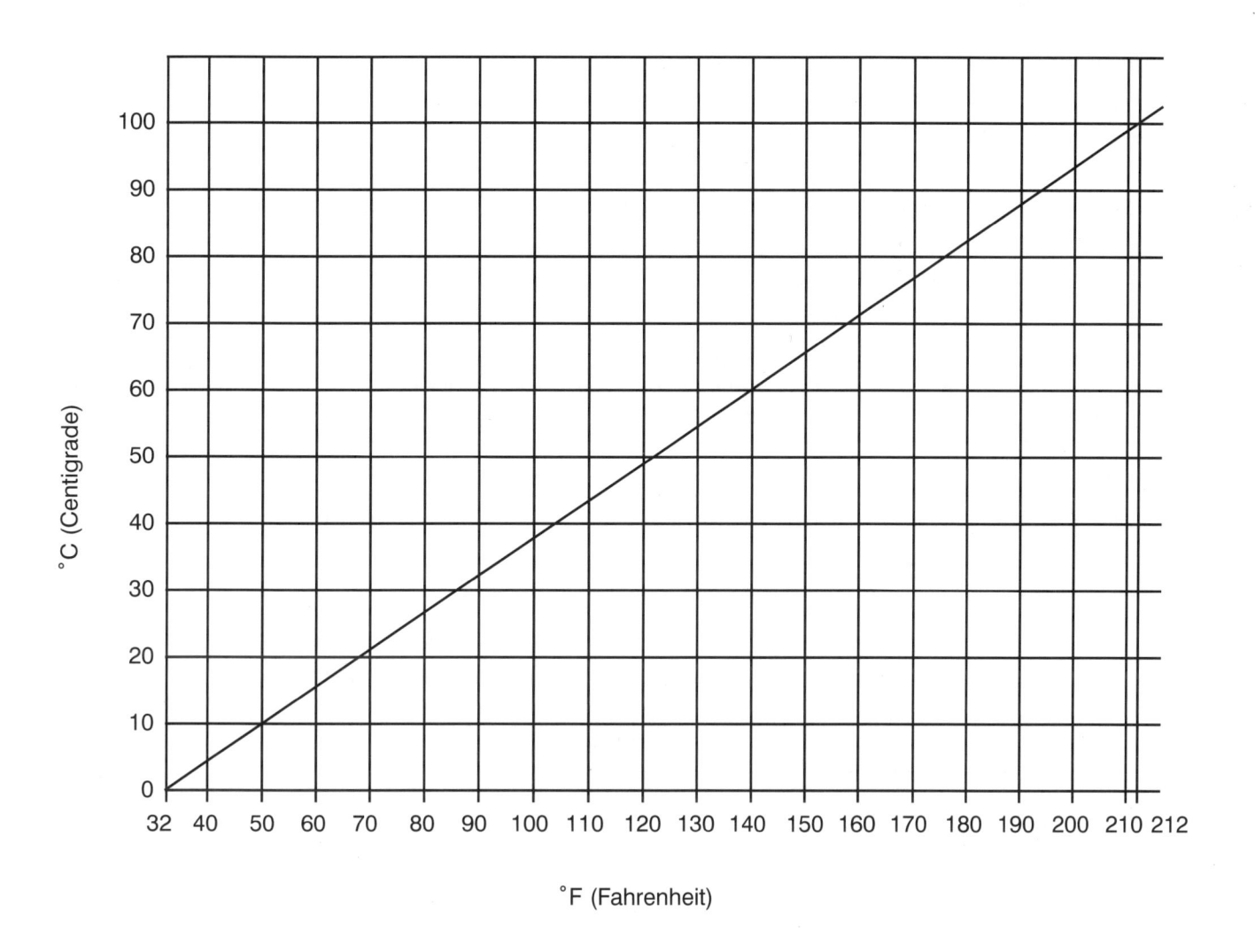

RESOURCE SHEET 40

[Graph showing conversion between °F (Fahrenheit) on x-axis from 32 to 212, and °C (Centigrade) on y-axis from 0 to 100, with a straight line]

°F (Fahrenheit)

Use the graph above to convert these temperatures.

°F	→	°C		°C	→	°F
212				75		
38.4				50		
60				5		

Hotel beds

All these problems involve adding and/or subtracting.
See how many you can tackle alone.
Leave those you have difficulty with for discussion in your group.

Hotels in a tourist town work out how busy they are by recording the number of beds booked as a percentage of the numbers of beds available.
Here are their results for one year.

January	46.2	February	63.3	March	66.9
April	76.6	May	75.06	June	73.8
July	74.1	August	75.2	September	81.7
October	79.6	November	72.1	December	55.0

1 In which month were most hotel beds full?

2 How many more per cent do the figures need to be raised to reach:

75% in November?

85% in September?

50% in January?

3 In which month were fewest beds taken?

4 What is the difference in the percentage of beds taken in these months?

January and September

March and December

July and August

February and May

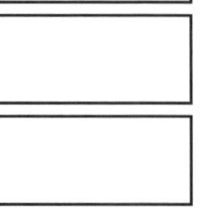

5 What are the percentages for January to March altogether?

Transport problems

RESOURCE SHEET 42

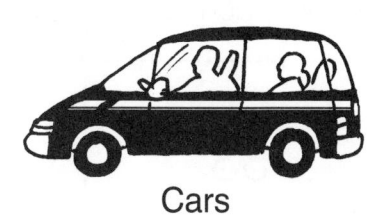

Bicycles   Buses   Cars

Try to solve these problems. Ask if you may do a calculator check of your answers.

1 There are 17 bays in the bus station. In one day 43 buses pull into each bay. How many buses run each day?

2 A car transporter has 9 cars on board. The driver needs to know the mass of his load. The cars weigh:

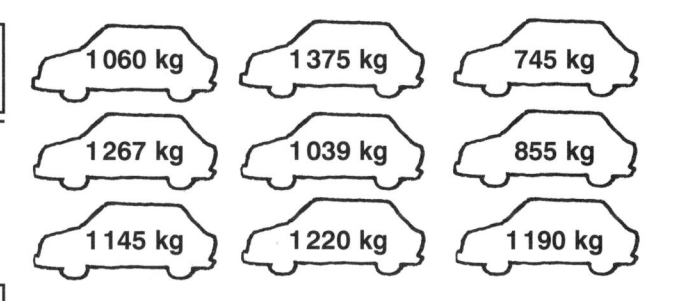

1 060 kg   1 375 kg   745 kg
1 267 kg   1 039 kg   855 kg
1 145 kg   1 220 kg   1 190 kg

3 Each of the "fast track" buses can seat 37 people. How many passengers could 98 buses carry?

a) What load is the car transporter carrying?

b) What is the average weight of a car (to the nearest kg)?

4 The fast track service, No. 16, to the shopping precinct, carries 13 056 passengers in one year. What is the minimum number of bus trips necessary to carry this number of seated passengers?

5 New cycle racks are being built. There are 13 696 individual spaces needed on racks each carrying 16 bikes. How many racks will there be?

6 2 020 000 litres of diesel are used on the No. 2 route. The diesel tank of a bus holds 400 litres. How many full tanks of diesel are needed for the No. 2?

7 An oil can for cycle use holds 25 ml. Simon needs 3.75 ml to oil his bicycle. How many times can he oil it from one canful?

Maths Action Plans, Problems and Data Year 6/P7 © David Clemson and Wendy Clemson, Nelson Thornes Ltd, 2002

121

Working with decimals

RESOURCE SHEET 43

Cut out each number card.

33	.6	.50	.06
270	.12	.18	.38
16	.78	.66	1.46 m
8	.34	.30	.62
150	.26	.42	.76
1370	.70	.72	.88
58	.82	.60	.80
99	.56	.22	.92
1	.02	.94	.4

Maths Action Plans, Problems and Data Year 6/P7 © David Clemson and Wendy Clemson, Nelson Thornes Ltd, 2002

Colin's commission

Colin is a representative who sells computer software and accessories. He is granted commission on his sales. The percentage commission varies.

1 On the first £10 000 worth of sales he is allowed 2% commission. How much is that?

2 On the next £5 000 worth of sales he is allowed 3% commission. How much is that?

3 Any sales above £15 000 attract commission at 5%.

This is Colin's annual sales record for 3 years. Work out his commission totals each year.

Year 1   £14 000

Year 2   £26 000

Year 3   £44 000

Commission totals

Year 1

Year 2

Year 3

Foreign currency

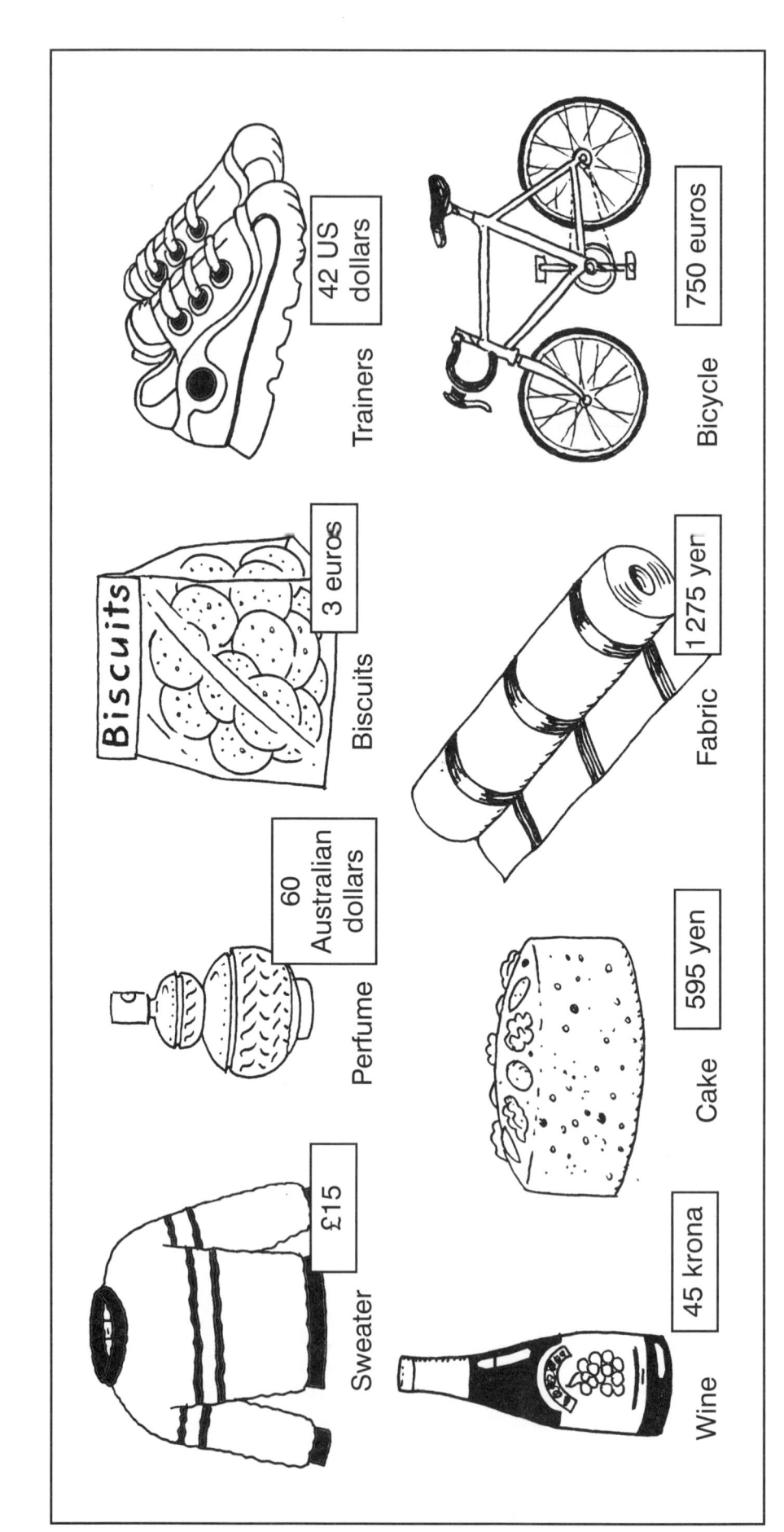

Sterling	Euros	Swedish krona	Australian dollars	Japanese yen	US dollars
£1	1.5	15	3	170	1.4

Trainers — 42 US dollars

Bicycle — 750 euros

Biscuits — 3 euros

Fabric — 1275 yen

Perfume — 60 Australian dollars

Cake — 595 yen

Sweater — £15

Wine — 45 krona

Percentage problems

Dine Out

1. Service charges are 10% in Dine Out. A pasta meal for four costs Jaswinder and Wasim £67. How much of this bill is the service charge?

2. With service included, Roland's bill came to £130. What part of the bill was the service charge?

   How much was the bill without the service charge?

Safehands

3. Safehands manage a block of flats where rents vary from £75 to £220 a week. Safehands charge 3% of the rent for their services. What would Safehands' charges be per week, ... for 4 weeks, ... for 52 weeks on these amounts?

Flat charges	Safehands' fee	
1 week	4 weeks	52 weeks
£ 75		
£150		
£180		
£220		

Dickens and Brown Solicitors

4. Mr Dickens helps Mr Batty to sell his house for £125 000. Mr Dickens' fee is 2% of the selling price. What is his bill?

5. To help Mrs Kelly with family business, Dickens and Brown charged £1 000 + VAT at 17½%. What did Mrs Kelly pay?

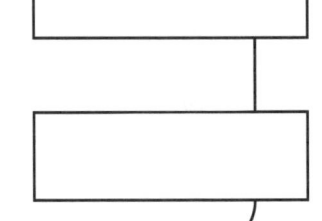

Brian the Builder

6. Brian put in a bathroom for the Taggart family. He charged £2 200 + VAT. What was the total bill?

7. Brian refloored Mrs Cousin's kitchen for £850 + VAT. What was the total bill?

Currency conversion

RESOURCE SHEET 47

Here are some exchange rates.

Sterling	Swedish krona	Australian dollars	US dollars
£1	15	3	1.4

1 Convert these prices to Swedish krona.

£2 [ ]   £12 [ ]
£4 [ ]   £15.50 [ ]

2 Convert these prices to pounds sterling.

a)
Swedish krona	Pounds sterling (£)
30	
45	
135	

b)
Australian dollars	Pounds sterling (£)
27	
12	
300	

c)
US dollars	Pounds sterling (£)
2.8	
7.0	
1400	
0.14	

3 Convert these prices to Australian dollars.

£1 [ ]   £15 [ ]
£6 [ ]   £13.50 [ ]

4 Convert these prices to US dollars.

£3 [ ]   £20.50 [ ]
£10 [ ]   £150 [ ]

Charts

Pocket money each week (class 6H)

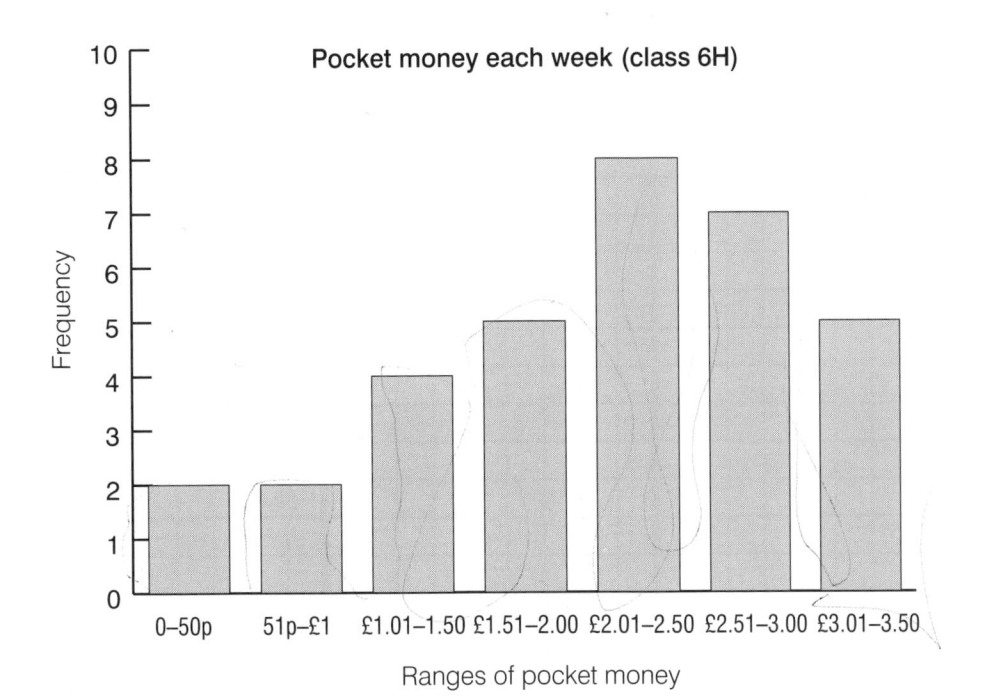

1. What was the range of pocket money with the highest frequency?

2. Which ranges of pocket money had the same frequencies?

3. Each week five children get the same range of pocket money. What is that range?

4. How many children were there in the class altogether?

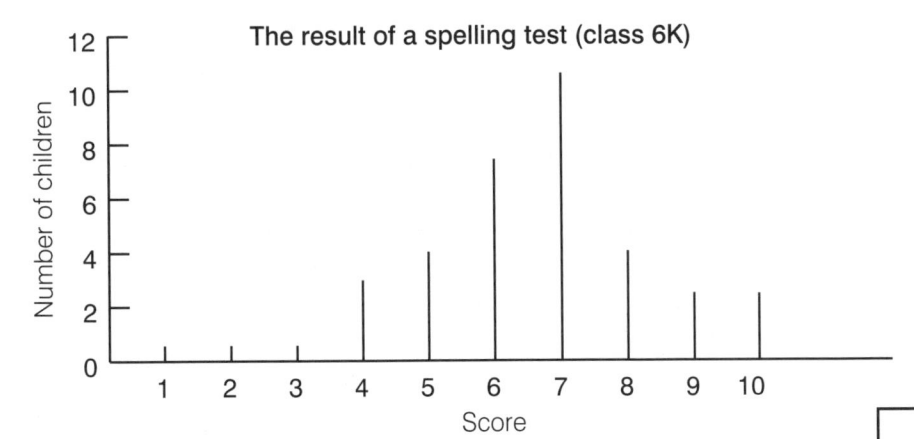

The result of a spelling test (class 6K)

1. What was the most common score?

2. What do we call the most common?

3. Which scores were achieved by the same numbers of children?

4. How many more children got 8/10 than 3/10?

Maths Action Plans, Problems and Data Year 6/P7 © David Clemson and Wendy Clemson, Nelson Thornes Ltd, 2002

A trip to the seaside

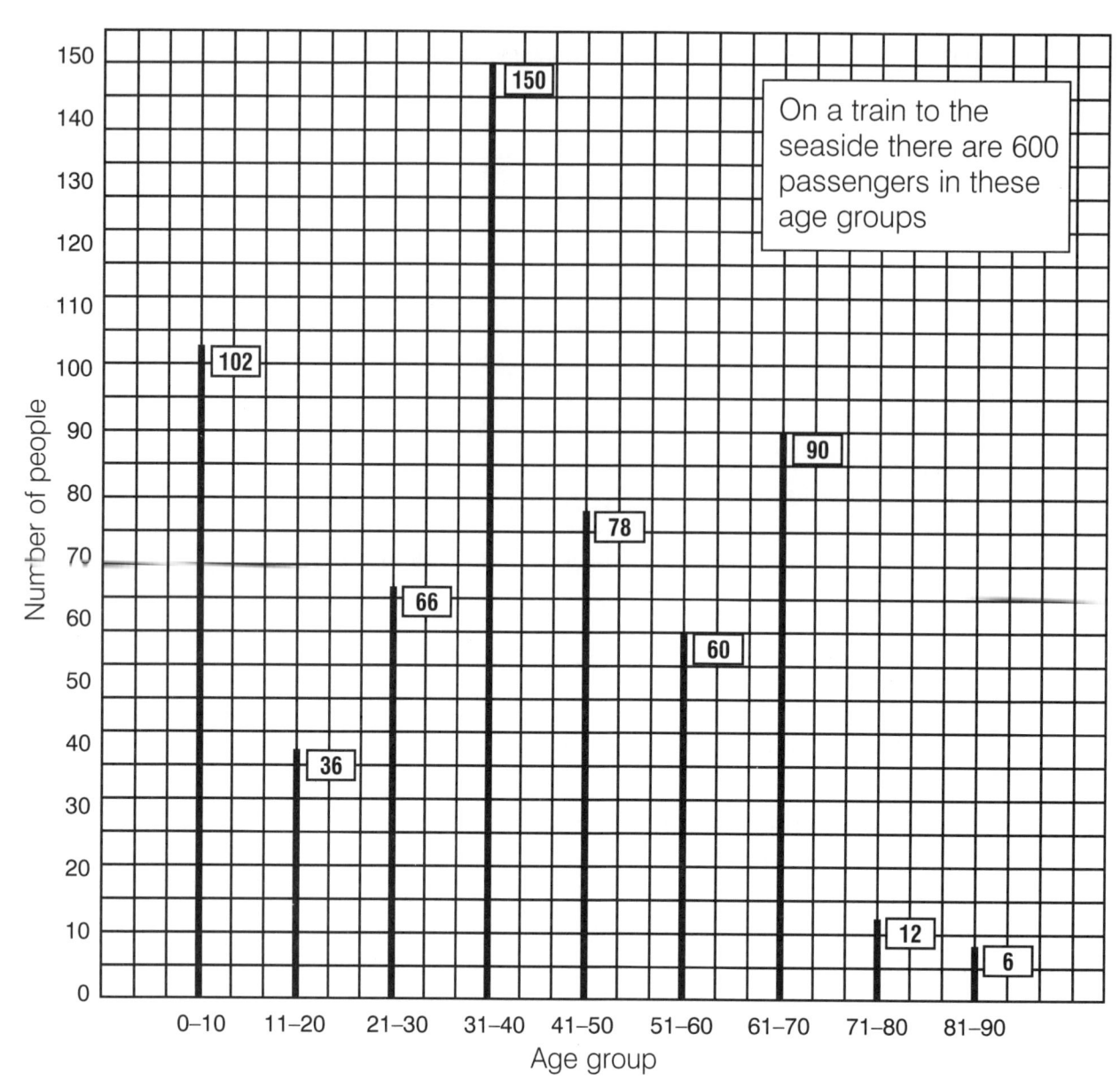

RESOURCE SHEET 49

On a train to the seaside there are 600 passengers in these age groups

[Bar chart — Number of people vs Age group:
- 0–10: 102
- 11–20: 36
- 21–30: 66
- 31–40: 150
- 41–50: 78
- 51–60: 60
- 61–70: 90
- 71–80: 12
- 81–90: 6]

The numbers at the top of each line show the exact number of passengers.

1. What percentage of the passengers were in these age groups?
   a) 11–20
   b) 31–40
   c) 71–80

2. What is the percentage of 51–60 and 61–70 year olds combined?

3. What is the lowest percentage on the chart?

4. What is the difference in percentage between the lowest and the highest age groups?

Holiday survey

RESOURCE SHEET 50

In a survey, 300 families were asked where in Europe they went on holiday last year. Here are their replies in percentages.

	%
Austria	6
Belgium or Luxembourg	4
France	23
Germany	3
Greece	10
Ireland	4
Italy	6
Netherlands	3
Spain	35
Switzerland	4
Other countries	2

1 Convert the percentages to actual numbers of families. Draw a bar line graph to show the data.

2 Write out the answers in full to these questions.

  a) How many families went to France? _____

  b) Which was the most popular destination? _____

  c) Which countries had the fewest families visit them? _____

  d) How many families went to Austria and Switzerland? _____

  e) How many fewer families went to Greece than to Spain? _____

Maths Action Plans, Problems and Data Year 6/P7 © David Clemson and Wendy Clemson, Nelson Thornes Ltd, 2002

Pie charts

RESOURCE SHEET 51

Trees and bushes in a wood

Softwood   25%
Hardwood   50%
Bushes   25%

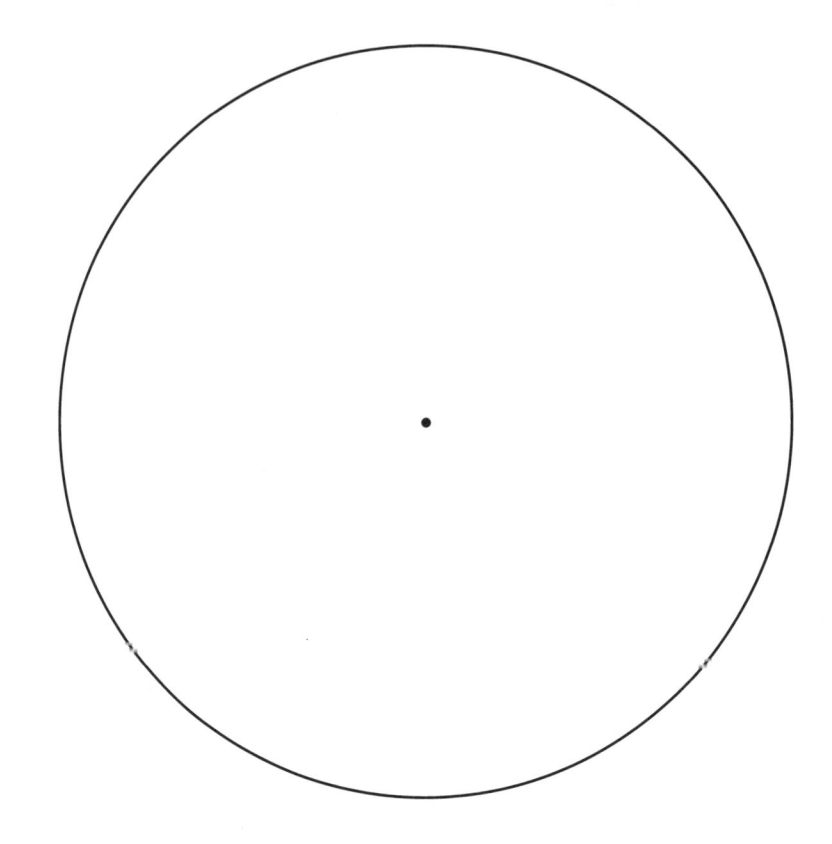

1 Draw one sector of 50% and two sectors of 25% each on this pie chart.

2 Draw your own pie chart to show six sectors – all of the same size.

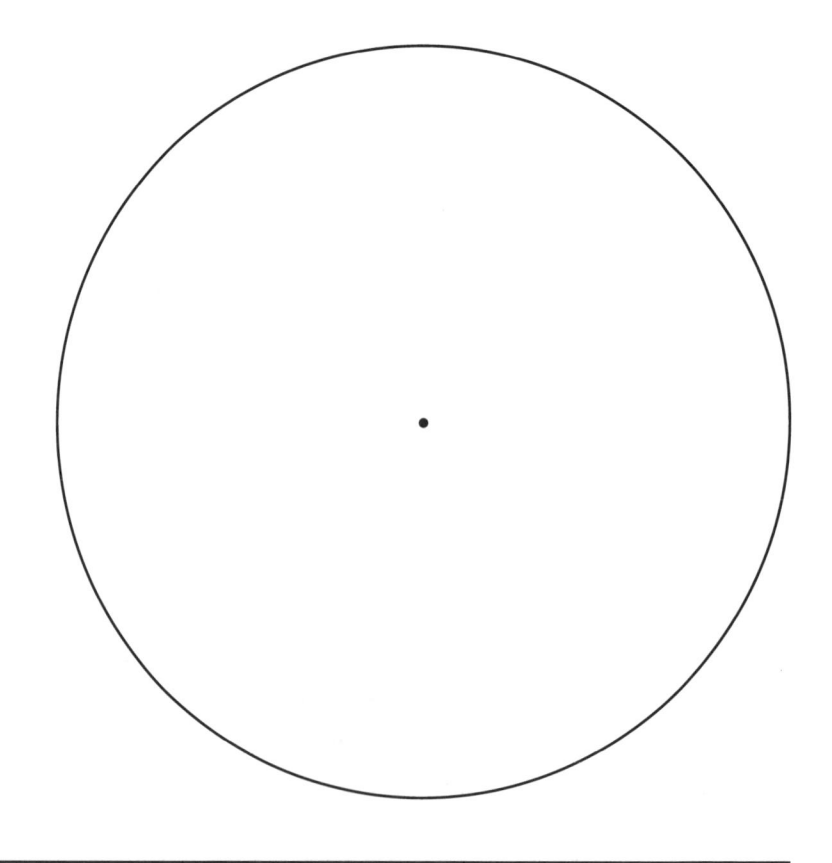

Sweatshirt sales

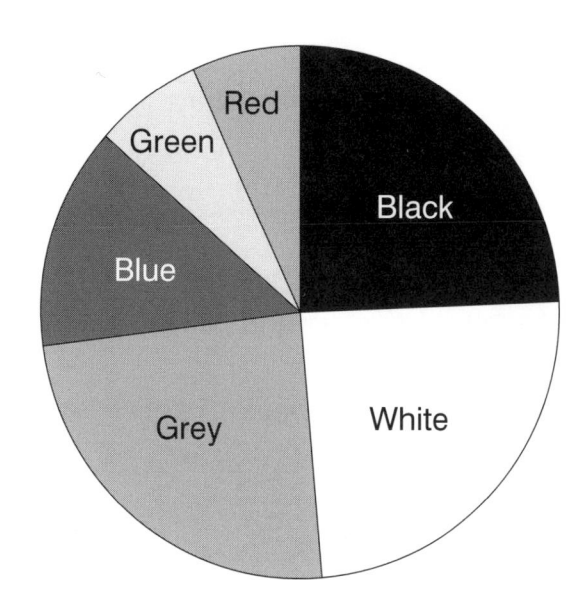

This pie chart shows the sweatshirt sales in **six** months, in one large store. Answer these questions.

1 The sweatshirts came in six colours. What were they?

2 What percentage of sales were white?

3 What fraction of sales were grey?

4 What percentage total were of black and white sweatshirts?

5 What fraction of sales were green?

6 What percentage sold were red?

7 If 80 blue sweatshirts were sold, how many sweatshirts were sold in total?

Sandwich sales

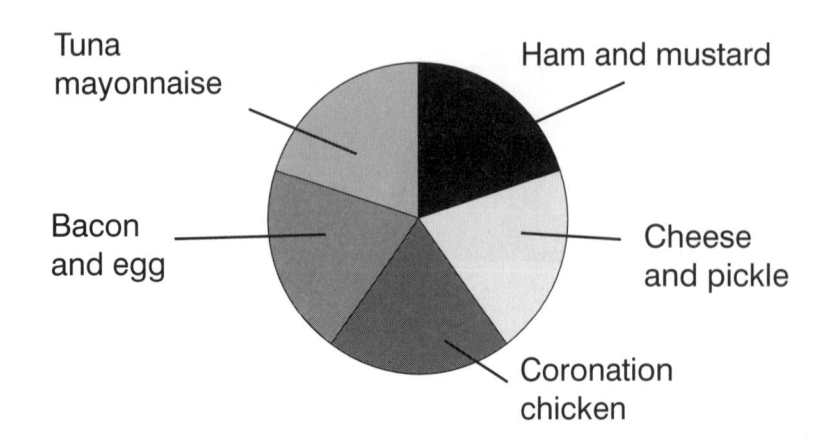

Tuna mayonnaise

Ham and mustard

Bacon and egg

Cheese and pickle

Coronation chicken

This pie chart shows sandwich bar sales of their filled sandwiches in a day.

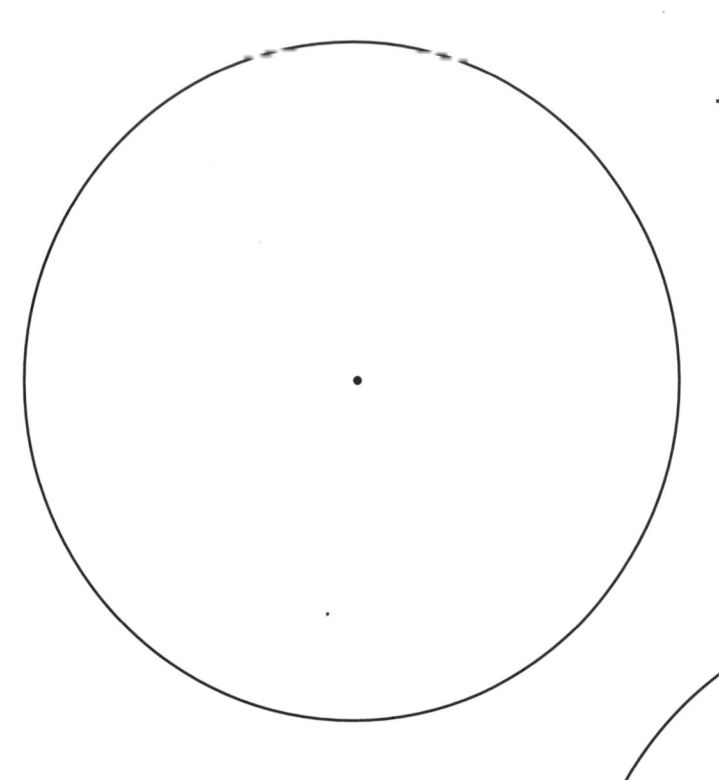

1 Make another chart to show the percentage sales if ham and mustard and tuna mayonnaise are halved and the other fillings are sold in equal amounts.

2 Ham and mustard was removed from the menu and smoked salmon put in its place. On one day smoked salmon made up 60% of sales. Each of the other fillings made up the same proportion of the remaining sales. Draw a pie chart to show this.

Mr Kipper's logo

RESOURCE SHEET 54

Don't get 'crabby' – come and eat your seafood at –
Mr Kipper's

Drop anchor at Mr Kipper's
We serve fresh Fish and Chips

Mr Kipper's
The best 'plaice' for Fish and Chips

Come to Mr Kipper's
for the freshest fish!

Something smells fishy!
he does chips, too!
..at Mr Kipper's!

KIPPER'S
Fresh K tasty
CHIPPY

Maths Action Plans, Problems and Data Year 6/P7 © David Clemson and Wendy Clemson, Nelson Thornes Ltd, 2002

Missing words

RESOURCE SHEET 55

Put these missing words in the sentences below.

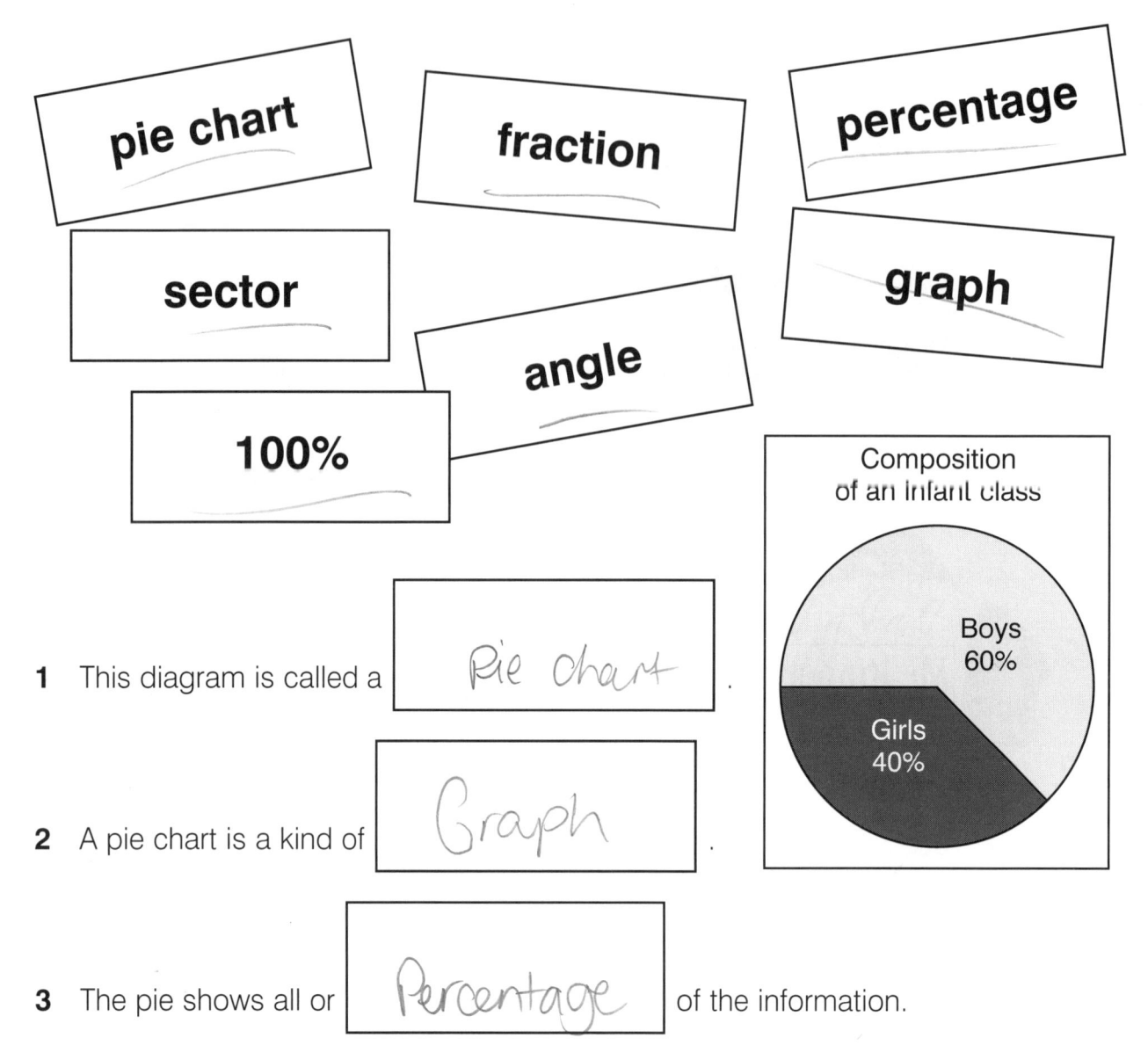

- pie chart
- fraction
- percentage
- sector
- graph
- angle
- 100%

Composition of an infant class (pie chart: Boys 60%, Girls 40%)

1. This diagram is called a [Pie chart].

2. A pie chart is a kind of [Graph].

3. The pie shows all or [Percentage] of the information.

4. Each slice of the pie is called a [Angle].

5. A sector shows a [fraction] or [100 %] of the whole pie.

6. The [Sector] of each slice shows its size.

What is wrong?

RESOURCE SHEET 56

See if you can spot what is wrong with each of these charts and graphs.

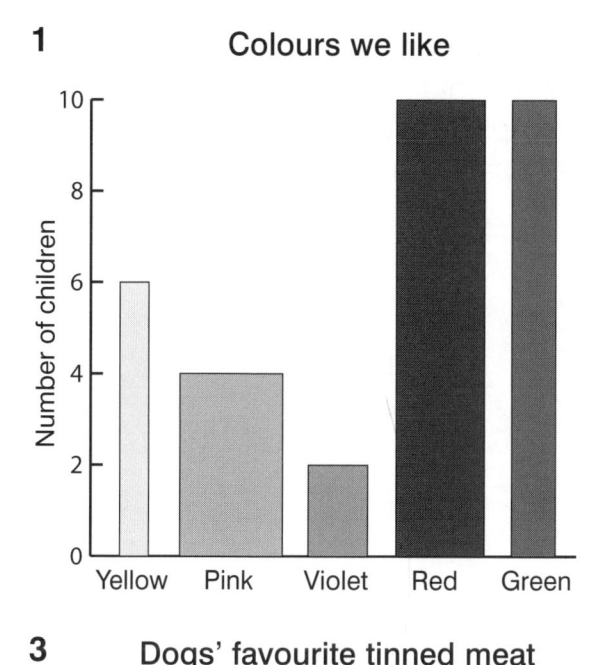

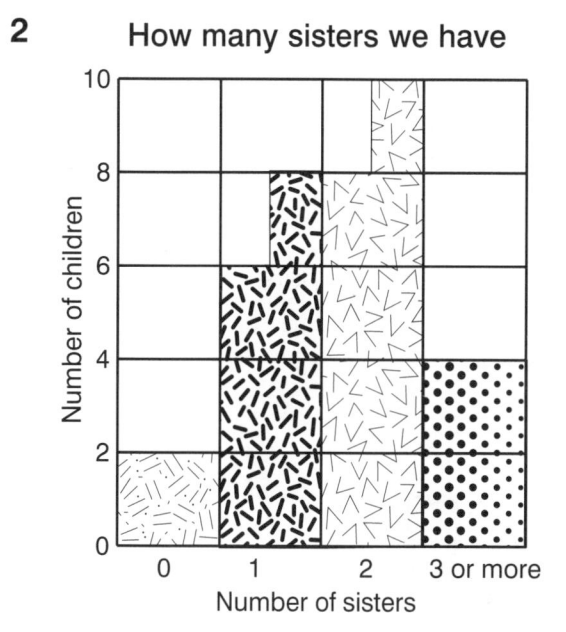

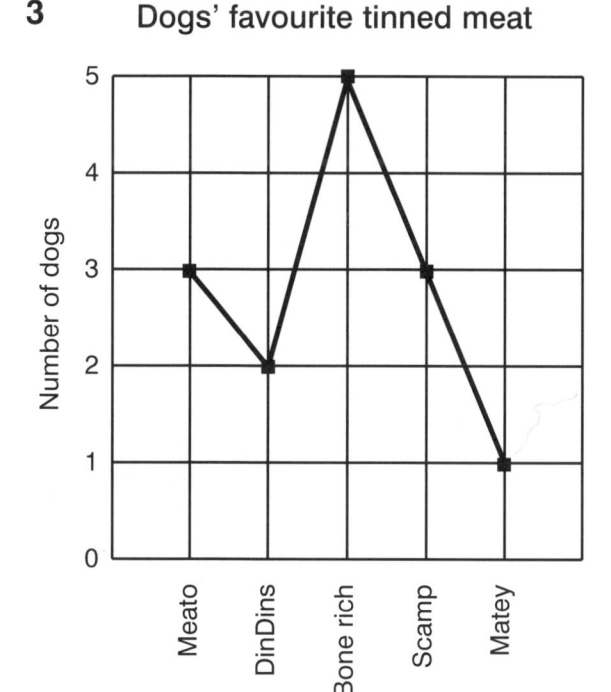

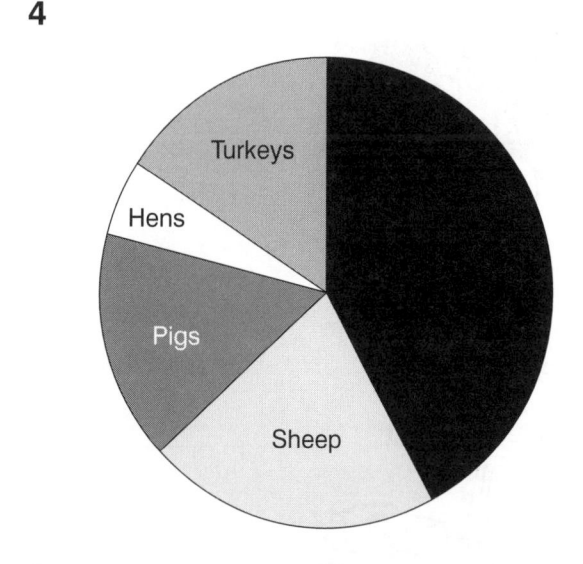

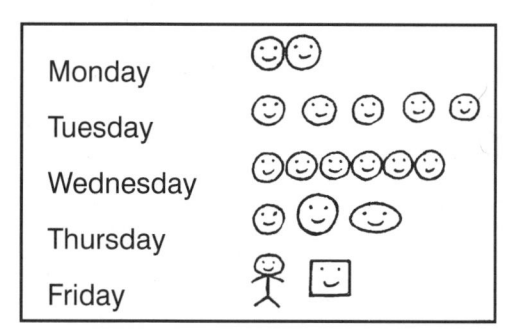

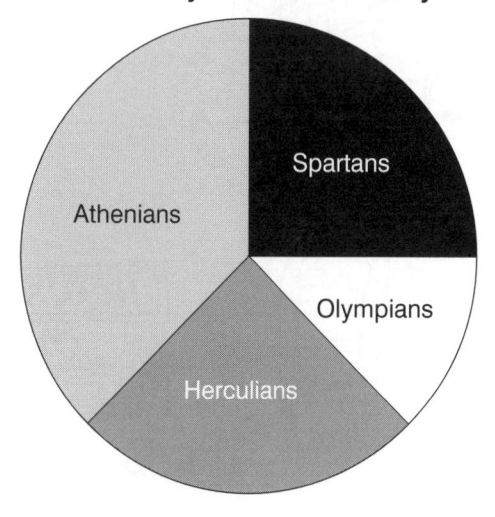

1 Colours we like

2 How many sisters we have

3 Dogs' favourite tinned meat

4

5 Smile stickers given out

Monday	😊😊
Tuesday	😊 😊 😊 😊
Wednesday	😊😊😊😊😊
Thursday	😊 😊 😊
Friday	🧍 ☺

6 Time taken by teams in a relay race

Maths Action Plans, Problems and Data Year 6/P7 © David Clemson and Wendy Clemson, Nelson Thornes Ltd, 2002

135

My survey

RESOURCE SHEET 57

Name _____

Look for "real data" in your home, garden or neighbourhood.
You need to find something where you can count the total, and also count the number in each group in the total. So, for example, if there are 56 flowers out in the garden, 14 blue, 27 red, and 15 pink ones, this is complete data that can be used in class.

Record your data here.

Capacity

A

cream: 142 ml, ¼ pint
milk: 568 ml, 1 pint
1 pint = 20 fluid oz

1 On the refrigerated shelf in the corner shop there are supplies of cream and milk. If the following supplies of the containers above are held, how much milk and cream is there? Give your answers in metric units.

6 cream and 8 milk: ☐ and ☐.

14 cream and 11 milk: ☐ and ☐.

2 There are also bumper cartons of cream available with 6½ times as much as the carton above. How much cream is this? ☐

3 There are 16 bottles in a crate. How much milk is that (in l and ml)? ☐

4 Mini-milks (one cup size) are also sold. There are 1.6 ml in each container. How many of these make a pint? ☐

B

Watering can: 2 gallons
Plant food: 500 ml

1 In spring, gardeners put 5 ml of plant food in every gallon of water. How many ml of plant food is put in two full watering cans? ☐

2 In summer they can use 7.5 ml to every gallon. How many full watering cans may be treated with plant food from a full bottle of plant food? (Give your answer to the nearest full can.) ☐

3 There are eight pints in a gallon. If the watering can is filled using a pint bottle how many bottlefuls will be needed for half a can? ☐

Three cans? ☐

Maths Action Plans, Problems and Data Year 6/P7 © David Clemson and Wendy Clemson, Nelson Thornes Ltd, 2002

Pools of water

1. A swimming pool contains 4 million litres of water. When it is 1/5 full how many litres are in it?

    What percentage of the contents is 600 000 litres?

    For cleaning it is filled with only 1/50 of its entire contents. How much water is this?

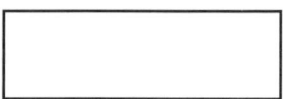

    If the pool is marked in eight lanes, how much water is in each lane?

2. The junior pool has 1.2 million litres in it. Write this number in numerals.

    The pool fills at the rate of 600 000 litres an hour. How many hours will it take to fill?

    Half the water in the pool is cleaned and returned to it. How much water is this?

3. A baby paddling pool holds 30 litres. If a bucket holds 1 gallon, how many bucketfuls are needed for the pool?

    If 650 ml of water is splashed out of the pool, how much is left in it?

World time zones

RESOURCE SHEET 60

Until the second half of the nineteenth century towns and cities in Britain had their own local times. Clocks in Penzance, Exeter, Banbury and London would be set to read different times.

A time standard called Greenwich Mean Time (GMT), set at the Royal Observatory in Greenwich, was introduced to help sailors and explorers to navigate the oceans during the 1600s. This did not become important to Britons on land until the railways were built. Imagine what it would be like if the clock at the station where you get on a train is set differently from the one where you get off. It would be impossible to have a timetable, or to know when to catch a train.

Greenwich Mean Time became official in Britain in 1880. All clocks in Britain then were set to the same time. GMT was adopted as the universal time standard in 1884.

An imaginary line, from the Earth's North to South Poles, drawn through Greenwich, is called the "prime meridian" (zero longitude). From this line time zones around the world are set. The line which is 180° away from Greenwich is called the International Date Line.

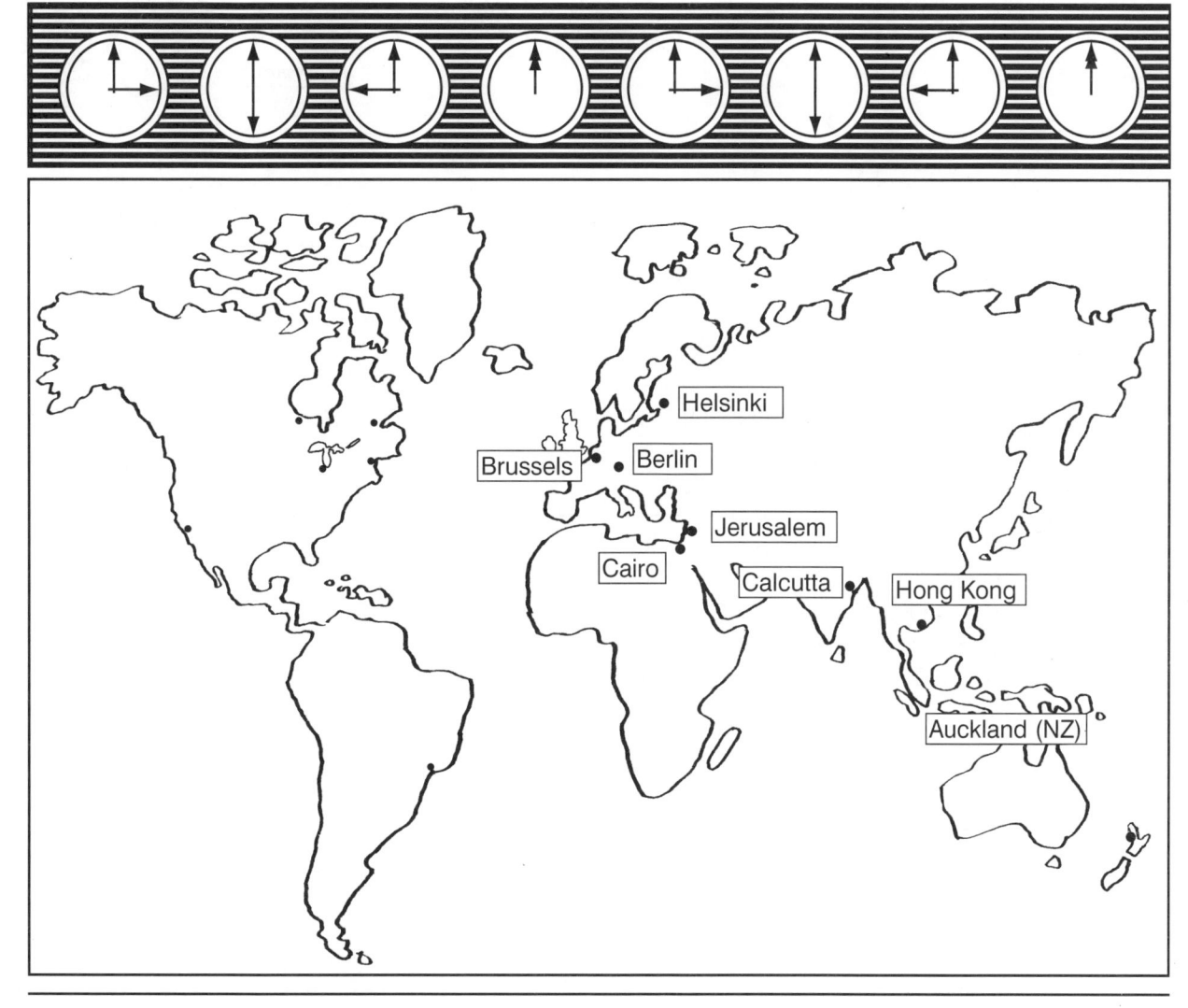

Maths Action Plans, Problems and Data Year 6/P7 © David Clemson and Wendy Clemson, Nelson Thornes Ltd, 2002

Time and place game

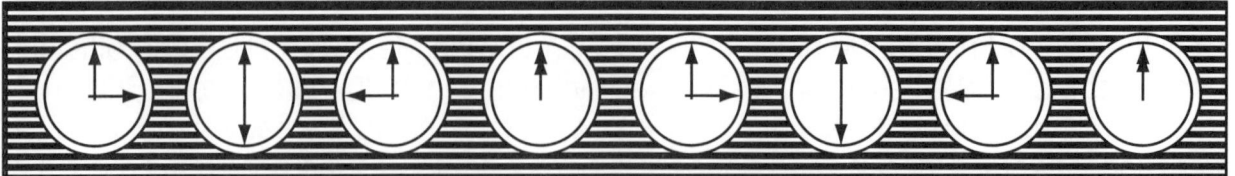

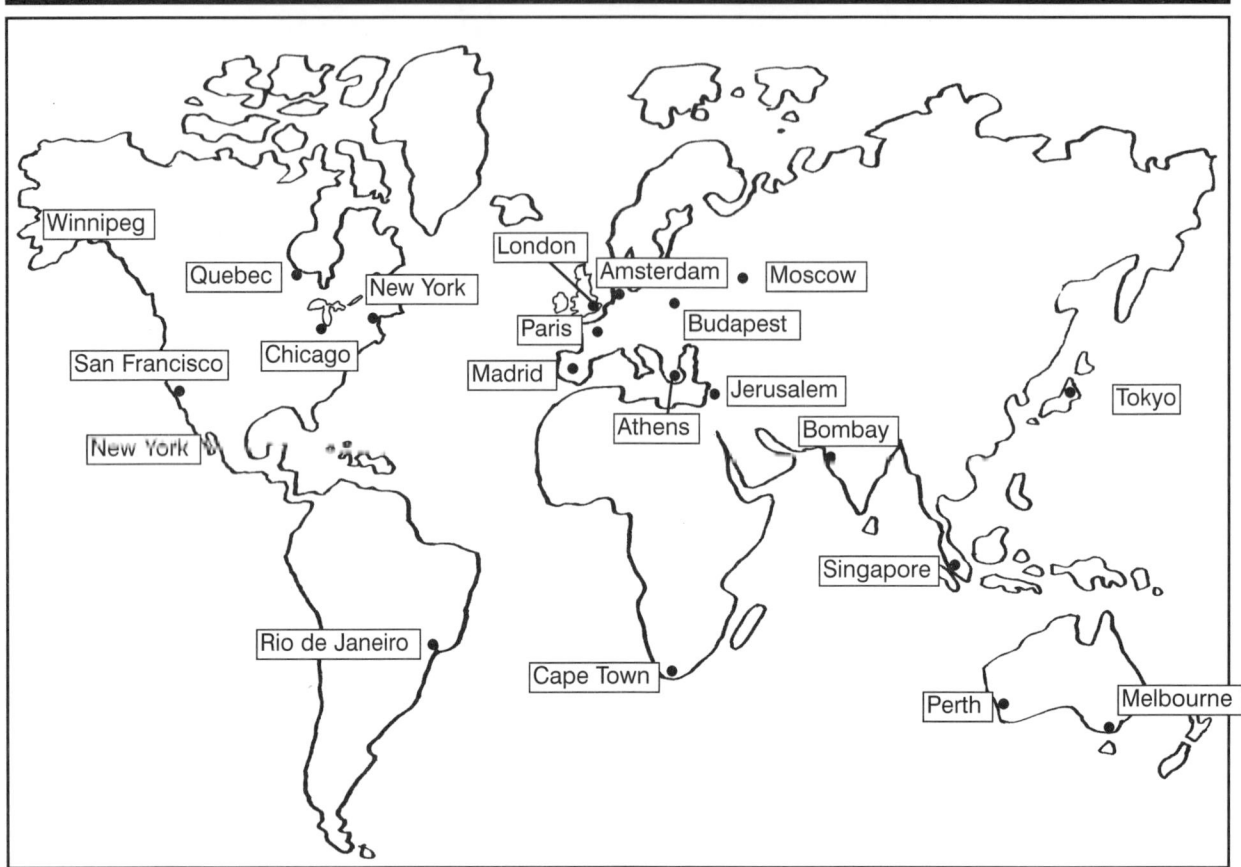

RESOURCE SHEET 61

Amsterdam	13:00	London	12:00	Quebec	07:00
Athens	14:00	Madrid	13:00	Rio de Janeiro	09:00
Bombay	17:30	Melbourne	22:00	San Francisco	04:00
Budapest	13:00	Moscow	15:00	Singapore	19:30
Cape Town	14:00	New York	07:00	Tokyo	21:00
Chicago	06:00	Paris	13:00	Winnipeg	06:00
Jerusalem	14:00	Perth (WA)	20:00		

This information is to help you when playing the "Time and place" game.

Maths Action Plans, Problems and Data Year 6/P7 © David Clemson and Wendy Clemson, Nelson Thornes Ltd, 2002

Time and place cards

RESOURCE SHEET 62

Madrid place card	Singapore place card	New York place card	San Francisco place card
London place card	Perth (Western Australia) place card	Rio de Janeiro place card	Winnipeg place card
Cape Town place card	Tokyo place card	Amsterdam place card	Jerusalem place card
Moscow place card	Melbourne place card	Athens place card	Budapest place card
Bombay place card	Chicago place card	Paris place card	Quebec place card

1:00 time card	5:00 time card	9:00 time card	13:00 time card	17:00 time card	21:00 time card
2:00 time card	6:00 time card	10:00 time card	14:00 time card	18:00 time card	22:00 time card
3:00 time card	7:00 time card	11:00 time card	15:00 time card	19:00 time card	23:00 time card
4:00 time card	8:00 time card	12:00 time card	16:00 time card	20:00 time card	24:00 time card

Maths Action Plans, Problems and Data Year 6/P7 © David Clemson and Wendy Clemson, Nelson Thornes Ltd, 2002

Selection of story problems

RESOURCE SHEET 63

1 Cross-stitch pictures need 487 "cross" stitches to make them. How many stitches are there in 19 pictures?

2 The garden wall needed 47 rows of 218 bricks each. How many bricks were needed?

If three rows of bricks were left how many is that?

3 Celia estimated that there must be about 1500 leaves on the young tree. As there are 16 main branches, how many leaves, on average, are on each branch?

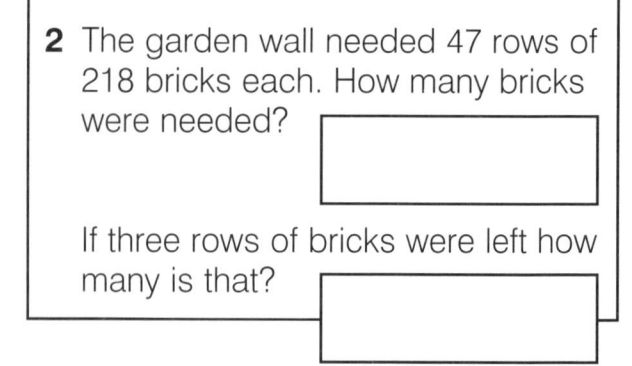

4 The library van delivers 1196 books for the 13 classes in a school. How many can each class have?

5 A teacher has 132 treats to put in goody bags for children in her class. She gives each of the 16 boys 4 treats. Then she gives each girl 4 treats too. How many girls are there in the class?

6 There are enough children in the school to make up 19 football teams with 2 reserve players for each team. How many children are there in the school?

7 The teacher looked at his smiley face badges and said, "I have only 2.5% left of my 600 badge order." How many badges was he looking at?

8 I am thinking of a percentage. It has one decimal place and is greater than 2.0% and less than 2.9%. What could it be?

What are these percentages of ten thousand?

9 Is it possible to have 110%? We say "he gave 110% effort", but can that be true? Write what you think and talk to your classmates about it.

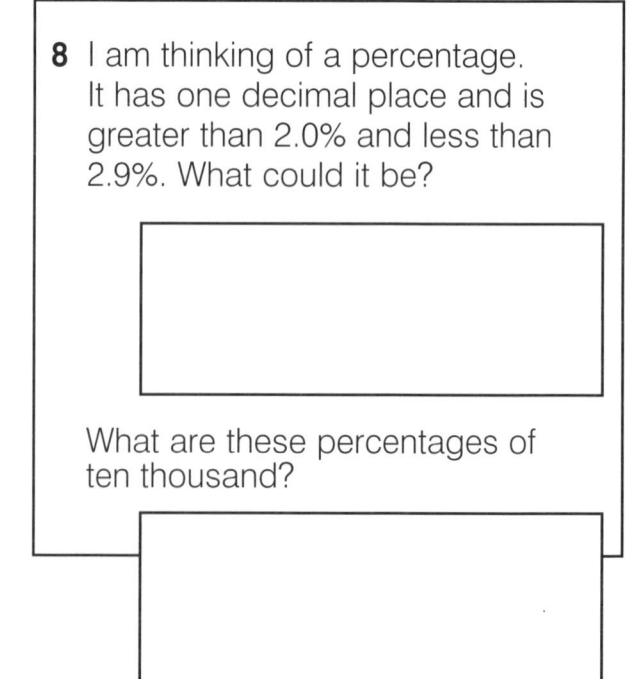

Maths Action Plans, Problems and Data Year 6/P7 © David Clemson and Wendy Clemson, Nelson Thornes Ltd, 2002

More story problems

RESOURCE SHEET 64

Solve these story problems. Write about how you worked them out.

1 There are 5000 pencils ready to pack in the factory. Lloyd thinks that makes 412 boxes of 12 pencils. Jade thinks it is more than that. What do you think?

Use this space for your working out.

Answer

2 There are 36 poster spaces along both sides of each of the 18 escalators. How many posters can be displayed?

Use this space for your working out.

Answer

3 In a spelling test these children got marks out of 30: Esme 22, Zena 27, Winston 19, Simon 23, Ali 9, Amy 23, Frances 20, Rhiannan 16, David 18, Chris 23.

What is the mode, median and mean of these marks?
Use this space for your working out.

Mean

Mode

Median

Maths Action Plans, Problems and Data Year 6/P7 © David Clemson and Wendy Clemson, Nelson Thornes Ltd, 2002

Problems for our teacher!

RESOURCE SHEET 65

Discuss how you would go about solving these problems.
For each problem list the tools* you might use, the operations necessary and an estimate of what you expect the answer to be.
How might you present your answer?

1. What were the savings on special offers in the week's shop?

2. How much paint is needed to paint the walls of your bedroom?

3. What is the growth rate of a kitten over six weeks?

4. What is the number of sheep in several flocks (each over 100)?

5. How many people live in your town and have size 10 feet?

6. How many trays of 12 × 12 eggs can be made up each day at the poultry farm?

7. What is the number of children likely to be in your school next year?

8. What is the length of a car journey across Britain through Manchester and Leeds?

9. How many budgies did the pet shop sell last year?

10. Do all packs of the same brand of cheese crackers have the same number of crackers?

11. How many glasses of wine can be poured from ten bottles of wine?

12. How many people locally went to the cinema last week?

*The tools might include things for measuring and/or a calculator.

My word problems

RESOURCE SHEET 66

Make up some word problems.

For example, for 30% of 518 you might write: Mrs Broodie kept chickens. She hatched 518 chicks and found 30% of them grew into cockerels, while the rest were hens. How many cockerels were there?

1   30% of 518 =   **155.4**

Word problem
```
 51.8
   3 x
─────
 155.4 ✓
```

2   8 × 74 =   **592**

Word problem
```
  74
   8×
─────
 592
```

3   650 × 3.2 =

Word problem
(scribbled working: 650, 3.2, 300, 520)

4   125 ÷ 0.25 =

Word problem

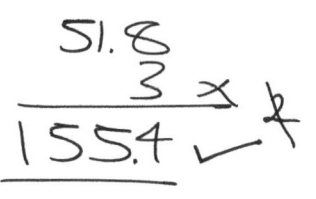

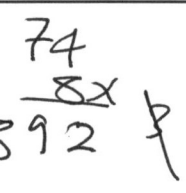

Now try to make up some word problems of your own that use both multiplication and division.

Spinners

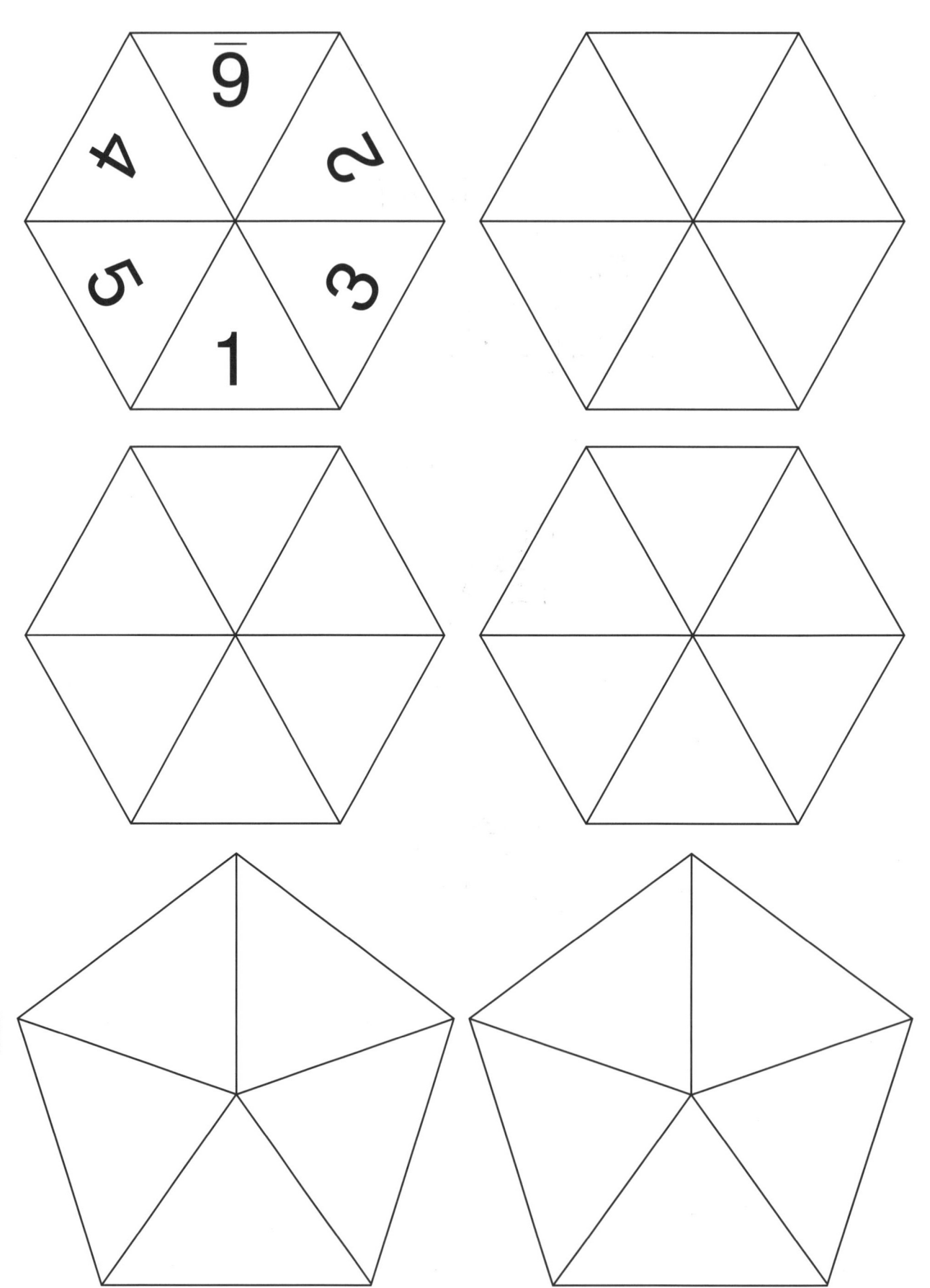

GENERAL RESOURCE SHEET A

Half centimetre squares

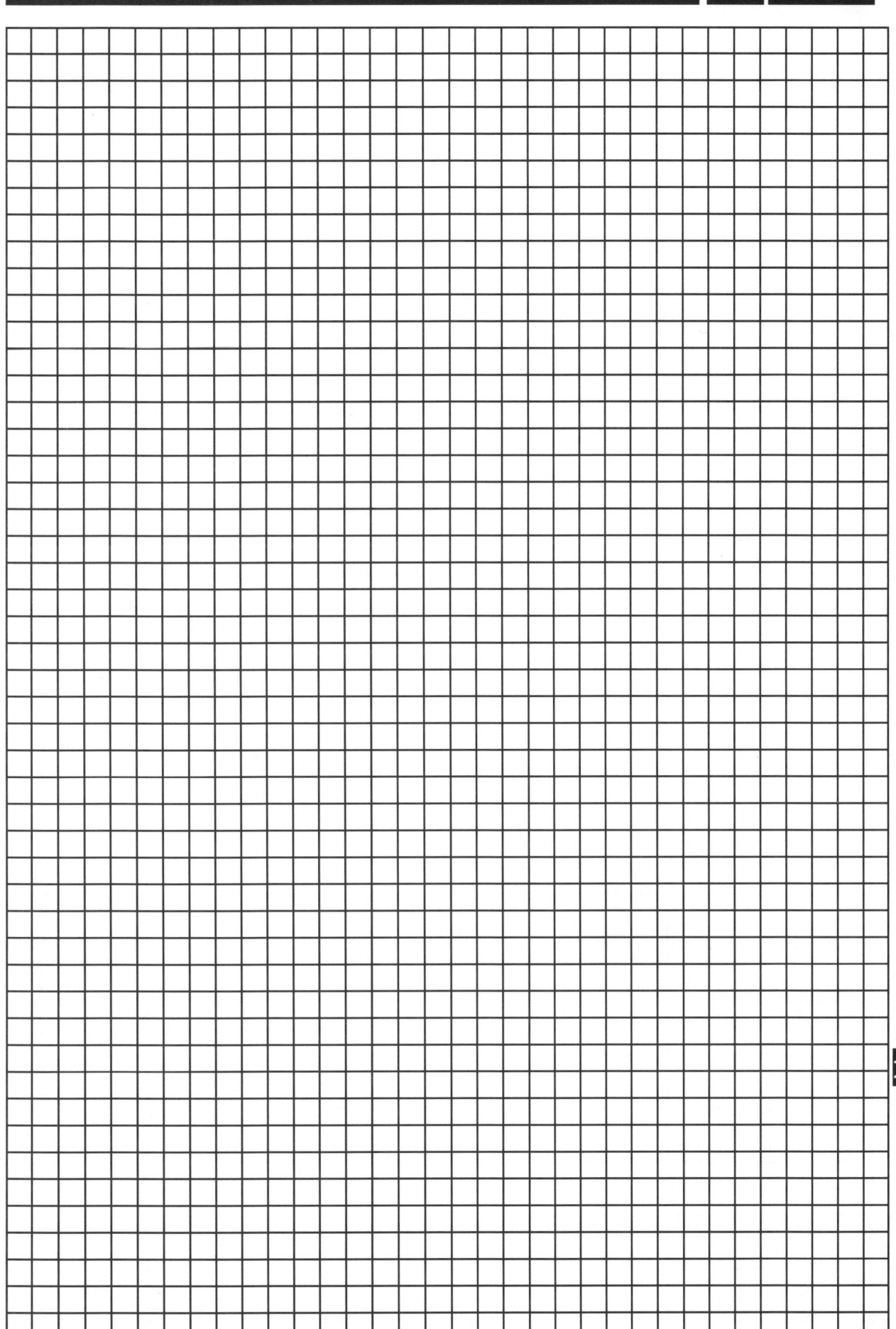

Centimetre squares

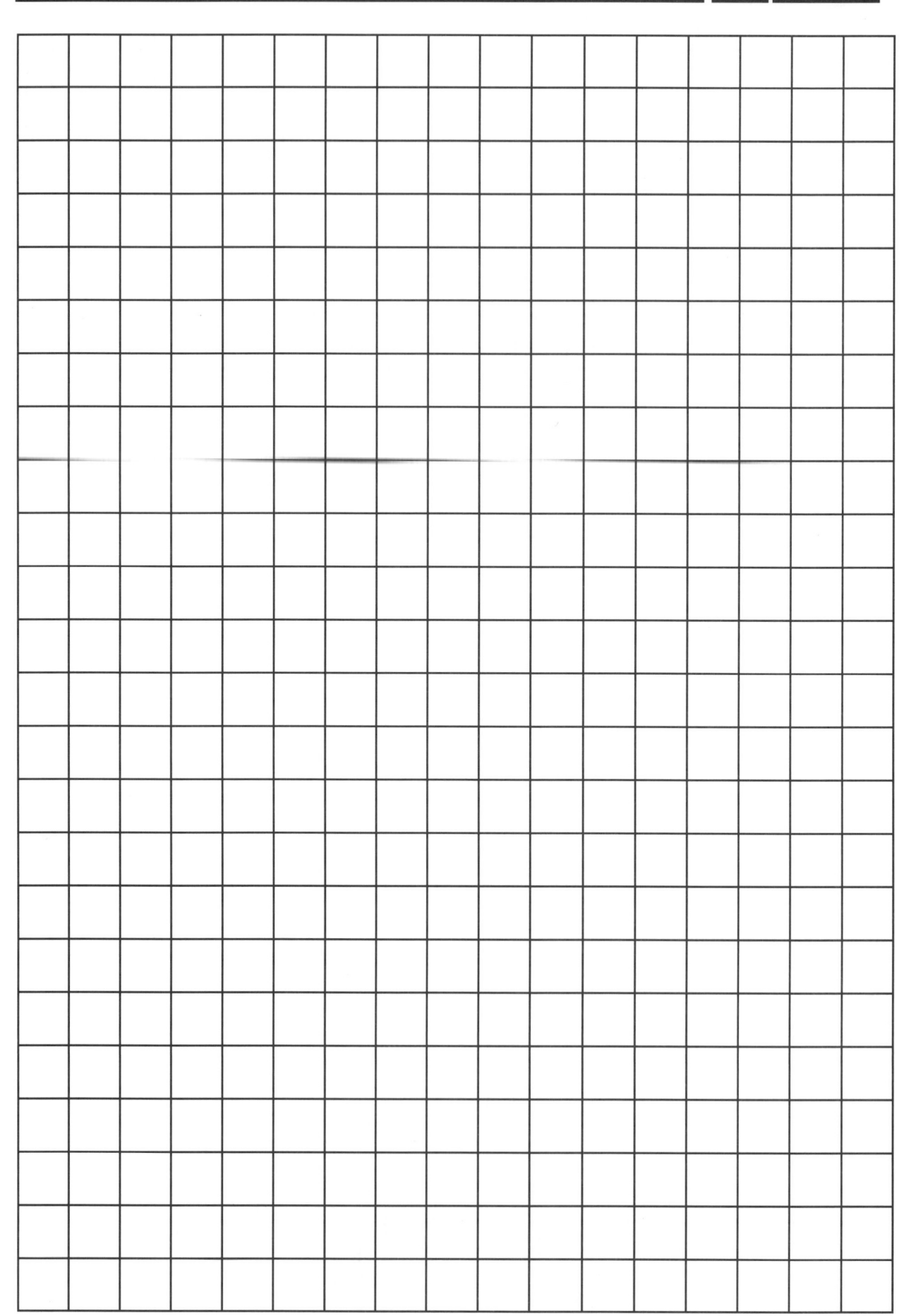

Graph paper (2 mm and 20 mm)

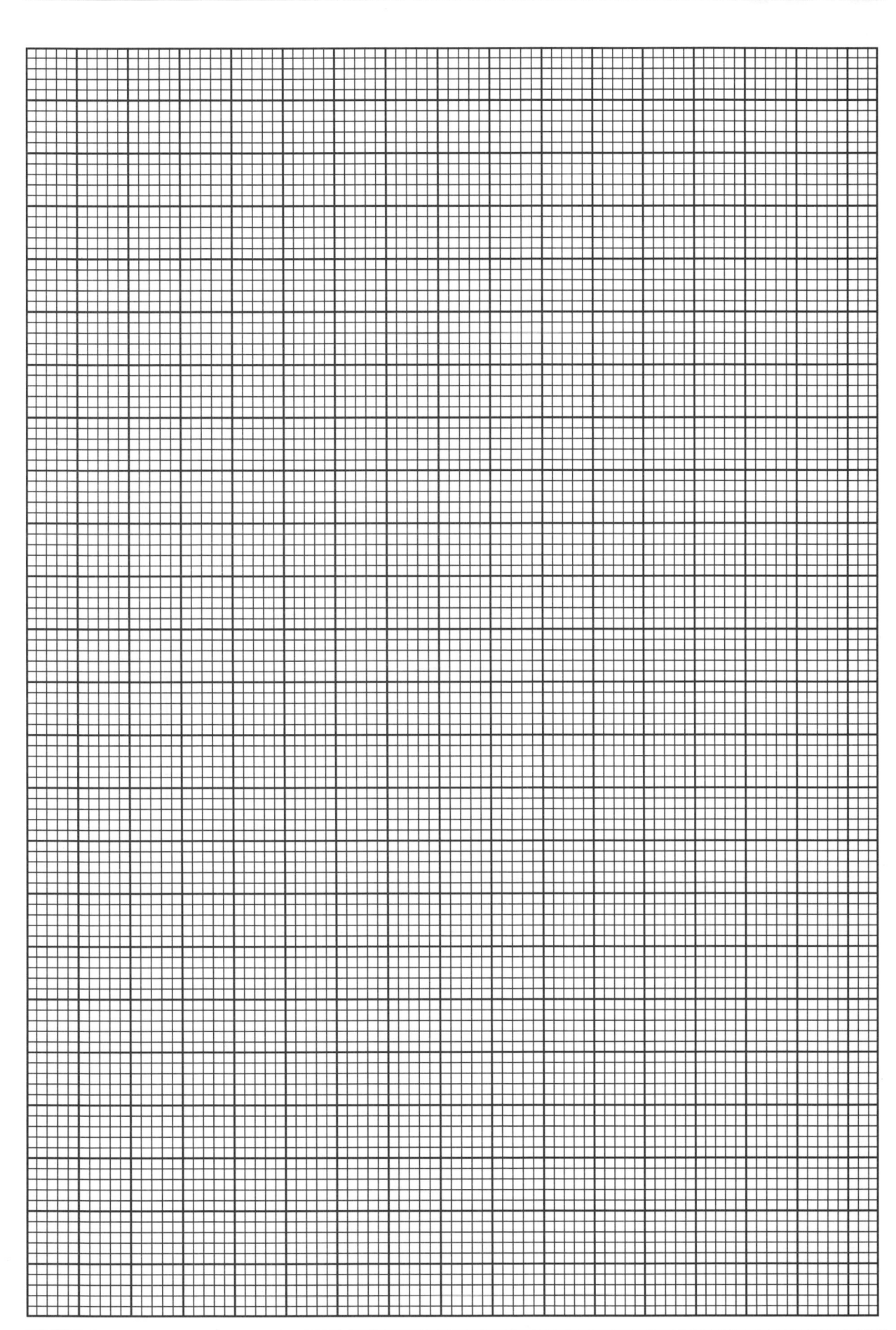

Pie charts

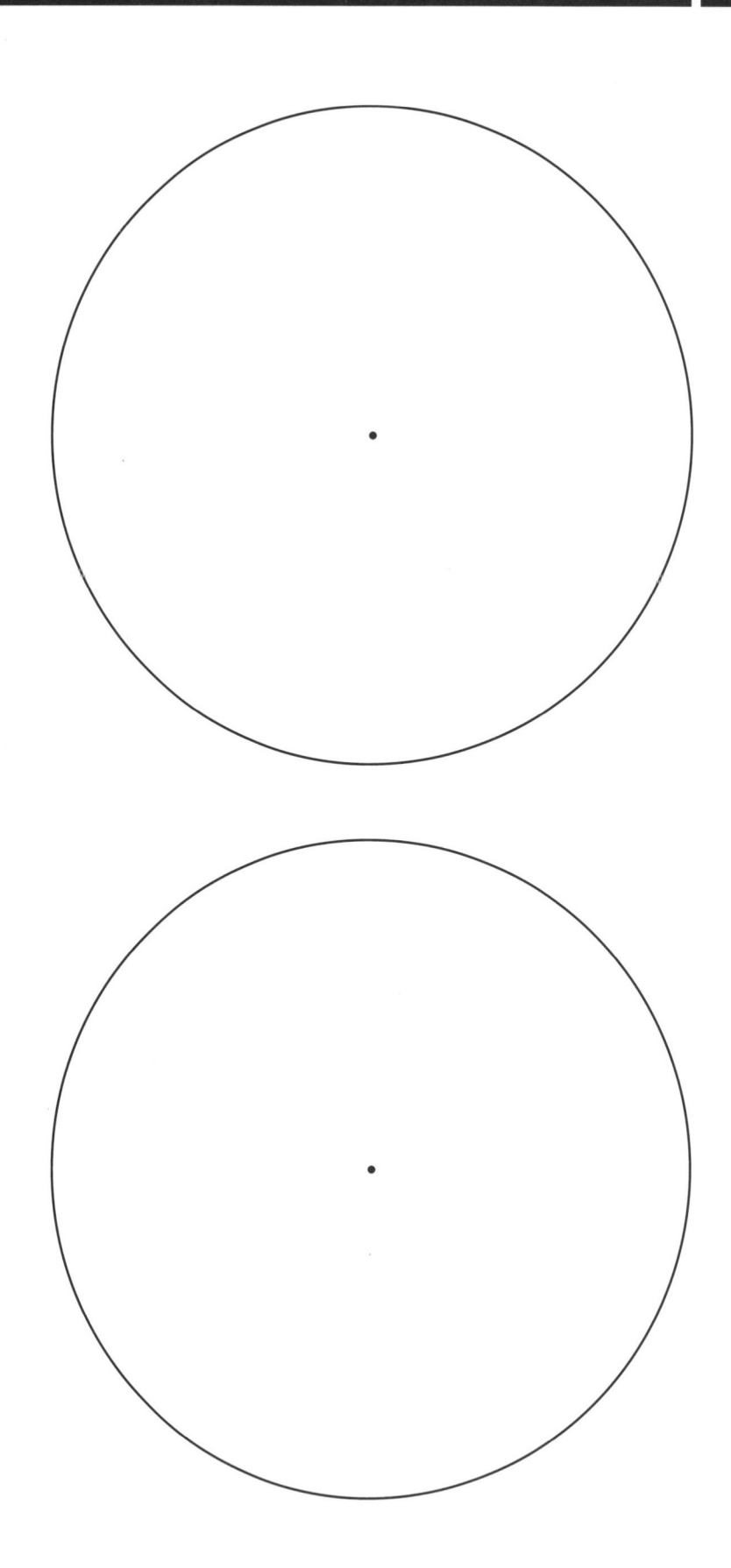

Small card grid

Digit cards

GENERAL RESOURCE SHEET G

2	4	7	0
2	4	7	0
2	4	6	9
1	3	6	9
1	3	5	8
1	3	5	8